CONVERSATIONS

THROUGH THE VENT

A GLORIOUS TALE OF REDEMPTION

Christopher J. Oaks

Brandon Nelson

Thanks for your support! # Everyone still hods Value! Christopher J. Oaks Thanks Brother!

Printed in the United States of America

First Printing, 2020

ISBN 978-0-578-78421-2

Published by: NS Publishing Company

www.theauthorstrategist.com

Table of Contents

Acknowledgements by Christopher J. Oaks

This has been a long and arduous journey to achieve transmogrification. There are many who have helped me on my path. I would like to take the time to name as many as the space will allow me to.

To my family, you have been my rock of refuge and never did you turn your back on me. You all believed in me when I did not even believe in myself. Many, many thanks for your unwavering love.

To my Mom, you are truly a blessing. Your love and sacrifices will not be in vain.

To my sister Krystle who has been something of a superhero to me. She truly deserves a cape. Love you forever sis.

To my Dad and Momma T, you were instrumental in my desire to change. You showed me the definition of unconditional love. The power of forgiveness is a true beauty.

To Elroy (pops) man I love you more than you will ever know. You are truly a good man! Nothing will ever change that.

To my aunt Dimples, who has become a great supporter and motivator, I love you.

To my Grandparents Grandma Terry, Papa Rib, and Grandma Chris. You are awesome and I appreciate all your wisdom.

To my Bro Timothy, you showed me how to beat the statistics. Recidivism is a thing of the past. Thanks for showing the way.

To my friend D Fresh. You are what a true friend looks like. Blood could not make us any closer. Thank you for the support over the years.

To the mothers of my children. I am in total gratitude for you ladies being good mothers and providing consistency, security, and nurturing where I could not. And to my children, Zachary, and Avery, you are my motivation and I love you dearly.

To the authors Mike Enemigo, Joshua Kruger, and James Allen. You all have shown me the way and opened my mind and heart to true freedom. Last, but far from least thank you God for saving me and giving me another chance. I will strive every day to stay in alignment!

I would also like to thank the following people for their support and contribution to this book. Your continued support is greatly appreciated.

Lashonda Suetopka, Destiny Carson, Adriane Thomas, Patricia Serrano, Shonnie Lee, Crecetta Herbison, Crockett Oaks., Elizabeth Shells, Vicki Gabriel, Antonio Garcia, Janice Campbell, Zora Moore, Denise Bouie, Pastor Elmer Gabriel, Wendell Edwards, Elease Jones, Yvonne Colley, Krystle Suetopka, Billionaire Brittany Priscilla Brown, Frances Watts-Levingston, Virginia Lozada, Deshana Matthews, and Mollie Thomas.

Conversations Through The Vent

Acknowledgements by Brandon Nelson

To my parents for the endless sacrifices they have made in order to see me to adulthood.

To all the friends that never lost faith in me even when I lost faith in myself.

To my son for being the driving force that changed my life for the better.

To my siblings who also inspired me to change my life in order to set an example.

To my Grandparents who have blessed me with the wisdom of generations both directly and indirectly.

And to God and the Universe for guiding my feet and correcting my steps when I began to wander and providing the resources and nutrients I needed to grow as a man.

"Until"

by

Christopher Oaks

Until you've been arrested and spent endless days in jail, and walked a hundred miles without ever leaving your cell...

Until you've lost your family and utterly alone, you try to seek comfort realizing it was left at home...

Until you've faced a judge and entered your guilty plea, and you've heard the words of judgment that you won't be going free...

Until your days turn into months and months turn into years, you lie awake at night and cry, shedding endless tears...

Until you've lost all hope and every dream you've ever had, you fight to keep your sanity in fear that you'll go mad...

Until you've gone through all these things and lost all human will, how can you look at me and say you know just how I feel???....

Until

Introduction

Conversations Through The Vent

In prison, when an inmate is sent to the "hole" for disciplinary infractions, he is left in a cell the size of a small bathroom. He is isolated from the general population and has little to no interaction with his family and friends on the outside world. In the hole, there is no TV, and the books are limited. If you do not have family support to send you books you won't have any. And for the most part, you are utterly alone. Inmates use their time in the hole in various ways. Some write letters, others sleep and workout, some go crazy, yell, kick, and scream, cuss the guards out and fight. Some cry and reflect on their lives and dwell on past failures. Others plan for the future. Some inmates make jokes to make light of their situation. In some extreme circumstances, inmates have even committed suicide. There are many different factors to determine one's mindset while in the hole. I, myself, have done a combination of all the above things at one point or another.

In every cell there is a vent that circulates all the airflow throughout the cells. Through that vent you can communicate with the inmates next to your cell or above you. Each vent is connected to four cells. Through those vents is where I found salvation.

I was able to communicate with others and for brief moments did not feel as alone. I have had some of the most critical and important conversations in my life through the vent. While in the hole and being at the absolute worst time in my life, I have come to the brink of insanity! Suicide was on my mind more and more often as the days turn into weeks, weeks turn into months, months going into years. I almost made the worst decision of my life. And that would have been to give up all hope.

As I grew in my maturity and faith, I understand now that God works in the most unforeseen ways. He sent aid and support to me where I felt I could not receive it. It all started with one conversation from the ventilation system.

Part I:

Sleep Walking

Chapter 1

Christopher

The Long Road to Hell

I often hear the same question being asked by many prisoners, "Do you think this was God's will to place us here to slow us down because we were moving too fast out there in the world?" I used to answer by saying, "Yes, everything happens for a reason." I now realize that was a bogus answer, and I just didn't want to take the responsibility at the time to hold myself accountable by saying, "No, God does not intend for us to be imprisoned. He did not place us here, we placed ourselves in prison."

As the bird was not destined to live in a cage, we were not destined for prison. It is only a consequence that derives directly from an action that we did. When you apply for a job, you now have the possibility of gaining employment. Same applies if you commit crimes, you now have the possibility of getting arrested. I've spent many years minimizing and blaming others for the reason why I ended up in prison. Although when I take a hard look into my soul and search for a clear understanding, the answer always comes back to only one person, me.

In 2015, I moved back to Oklahoma from attending college at Sam Houston State University in Texas. I made terrible decisions in

Texas that resulted in me going back to my home in Oklahoma City where my mother lives. I had no money, no job, and no direction of what to do with my life, so I fell back into old habits in obtaining fast money by selling weed. (Keep in mind this was before it was legalized). I didn't know anybody in Oklahoma besides family, so that was my motivation to get a job. I wanted to network, meet new people, and obtain customers to sell my weed to. I secured employment at a local Party Galaxy and worked there for a little while and sold weed at the same time. I came to Oklahoma with 2 lbs. of weed. I had no connection due to the fact I got into a beef with my connection in Texas. Once I sold out, I needed to find another source to keep my weed supply consistent. I picked Colorado to go and search for a new supplier. I took a few days off of work at the party store to fly to Denver, CO. Just after two days, I achieved my goal and found what I came for.

As the weeks went by, I got into a comfortable routine and decided I no longer needed the job. I was working part time and was even offered a permanent position but turned it down because I viewed working more hours as taking away from my hustle. I was making 10x my paychecks and working a job didn't sound appealing to me. I linked in with enough people and parted ways with the job. I just wanted to lie around with women, smoke weed, and hustle. I had no other real ambitions. One day I got too comfortable. I was riding in the car with a young woman and we were pulled over for a one-day expiration on my paper tags. I had weed in the car and therefore went to jail with a charge of possession with intent. I made bond and was eventually released. Upon release, I felt as if I needed to just move smarter and hustle harder so I can pay for my attorney. I continued going out of town to get my weed and I continued as if the case I had was petty. My thinking was that "It's just weed, it's not that serious. I'll just get a slap on the wrist." When it was time to go to court, through my attorney, I plead guilty and accepted the plea of 10 years' probation.

I was addicted to the lifestyle and the comforts that selling drugs provided me, so I saw no need to stop what I was doing. I kept living that self-destructive, fast money life until I got pulled over. This time in Kansas. I had 1,500 bottles of edibles in the car. Edibles are THC candy. At this point I panicked a little because when the officer found the edibles it was enough to arrest me. I wanted to fight the charge in Kansas. The officer lied about "smelling weed" and me "speeding" to justify a probable cause search of my car. I was not speeding, and I didn't even have weed in the vehicle, but when the officer found the edibles, it was enough to arrest me. I received the charge of distribution and bonded out of jail in Kansas. I went home to Oklahoma City. I couldn't stop the cycle of selling drugs. The more I felt I needed to grind to climb out of my hole, the bigger the hole got

My parents kept telling me "enough is enough and to stop with the bullshit, you've tried it and it's not working, give it up!" I remember my mom telling me that and I just took that as a challenge. I was only looking at the error that got me caught up for that particular time and not the picture as a whole. I also was involved with a woman I should have never been with. My mom, dad, sister, and friends told me she was no good for me. She was nearly 20 years older than me and she applauded my hustle and cheered me on. I got blinded by the way she would give me her entire taxes so I could re-up and get multiple pounds. It was to the point where I was getting 10 to 15 thousand at a time and I never saw that type of money before.

I worked a deal with my lawyer in Kansas to just get a 3-year probation deal and had the foolish mindset that no one could tell me nothing. I got big headed. I was doing my thing. Even though I hit a couple of bumps that come with the game. And I felt as if the probation was no big deal. I was listening to trap rap, buying expensive cars, messing with several beautiful women, seeing my son, and doing for him, travelling and shopping with my "trap queen" Deidre. I would like to say she had me brainwashed but that's not accurate. I was blinded by my own foolishness and ignorance.

Here's how things got really bad for me. I purchased a 1-bedroom Condo that no one knew about so I could have affairs with other women besides Deidre. She caught me by following my car without me knowing to my secret pad. We had a huge fight over it, and she said to me "I made you. And if you think you can play me, I will break you as well." I dismissed it as an idle threat that was meaningless. We eventually made up and she "forgave" me for the Condo incident. I was doing business with an old high school buddy of mine and he would do favors for me such as, going out of town to pick my loads up for me so I no longer had to assume that risk. I had a court date in Kansas to finalize my probation deal, so I needed him to get my load. While I handled this court date in Kansas once and for all. All goes well with my probation deal and when I met back up with my friend in Oklahoma City, we took a drive in my car to go drop some smokes off across town. While in route, I get pulled over for not making a complete stop at the stop sign. My friend had 1 ounce of weed on him and he put it under his seat. When the police searched my vehicle, they recovered the weed and charged me with the weed. My friend was in the military and when they discovered this, they decided to put the charge on me and give him a break. Since I had a history of drug possessions (marijuana) they were more than willing to charge me with the weed that clearly wasn't mine, and along with that they confiscated $2,500 I had on my person. Now instead of the misdemeanor it was bumped up to a felony because of the money. Even though the money had no connection to the small amount of weed.

I once again went back to the county jail. I left my friend Deidre's number and told him to have her come get me out of jail immediately. She bonds me out of the county jail and I now have an additional weed charge to deal with. When I got back to the house Deidre and I shared, I was surprised to see my friend there. I asked him why he was here so early, and he told me that Deidre let him crash on the couch last night because they knew I would be back out on the street the following day. She saw no need to have him commute all the way back out to Lawton where he lived when we still had business to take care of. It didn't sit right with me because I know damn well, he could have gotten a hotel room. I voiced my displeasure at the decision to allow him to stay over in my absence. She thought it was amusing to see me jealous and she just gave me a sarcastic smile and replied, "ok daddy anything you say." I just dismissed it and moved on with other matters at hand.

Two weeks go by with no incident and it is time to re-up again. Deidre and I are at the studio apartment packing bags preparing to go on another out of state trip and she tells me out of the blue that my friend will be back in town the following Friday to pay me for what I gave him on consignment. I immediately get suspicious and ask, "why in the hell are you two texting?"
"He had your number for one reason only and that was to inform you that I was in jail and needed to be bonded out!"

"That was two weeks ago so again I'm not feeling the way you're maneuvering and if one more thing comes up about you and my homeboy, I'm gonna be trippin!"

"Delete the number now!" I impatiently barked at her. I just can't shake the feeling that she was on some funny business with my man and I didn't like it at all. She replied

"Ok, damn, why are you getting all out of character when it comes to your friend? I don't want him, ok so you can just quit trying to make something out of nothing."

"I'm not going to get back at you like that over the condo."

That was a dead giveaway. I never mentioned the fact that I felt she was trying to get me back for having the condo. Those were her words and she brought that up on her own. So that told me for sure she was up to something shady, she was just playing defensive because I had no definitive proof. That was one thing I didn't like about her character but ignored it at the time. She had the tendency to think because she was older than me, she could handle me anyway and run game on me. As if I didn't know any better.

I tried to ignore my growing annoyance with her and focus on getting the hotel booked in Denver. I tried to tell myself well I cheated on her as well, so I really couldn't hold her to a standard that I myself don't even live up to. That sounded like the right way to analyze the situation, but my heart was not agreeing with what my mind was telling me because at the end of the day, I never messed with any of her friends. That's a different kind of sting. I just couldn't let it go and about an hour later, I asked her if she deleted the number and to let me see her phone to make sure. I told her if she is playing a game with my boy, that's crossing the line and I would leave her, and the relationship would be over and that's for certain. She assured me the number was deleted. She said it with so much conviction as she unlocked her phone urgently trying to hand it over to me. The act was so good I almost just said never mind because she was so overly confident like she just couldn't wait to prove me wrong. I didn't want to run the risk of looking like a jackass and seeming jealous, so I almost just said "forget it." At the last minute I decided "the hell with it". I am going to check it out anyway. I'll rather trust my eyes than her lies. I scrolled and looked for the D's and his name wasn't there. My boy is originally from Miami and his area code to his phone number was a 305-area code. I typed in 305 and a name pops up. It said Denise. I knew it in the pit of my stomach, something was up. This local, country Oklahoma woman doesn't know anyone in Florida, let alone Miami. I was livid!

"So, Denise huh?"

"Ha-ha, so you think you got it all figured out?"

"The ole switch a rue with the name like I'm just the dumbest ass around?" She just looked at me with a dumbfounded expression like she couldn't think of any smart replies.

"Baby it's not like!" she started to protest.

"Listen save that weak ass shit for someone else I'm absolutely cool on you; this relationship is over!" I told her.

I began trying to grab my duffle bags so I can continue the trip alone. I told her to get out of my apartment and I'll swing by to get my stuff out of the house in a few days when I get back. I tried to walk around her so I can put some space between us. She wouldn't let me walk away from her and kept trying to block the doorway so I couldn't leave. She kept repeating "it's not like that." and that I'm "taking things out of context." I wasn't trying to hear anything she was saying. I open-hand slapped her and moved her out of my way. I will never try to justify what I did, but my objective in writing this book is not to manipulate the narrative to shed no blame on myself and not to take responsibility. My purpose is to lay out the events as they were by giving you the most accurate details as possible.

I sincerely and deeply regret that moment of weakness, but again I must be honest as possible. That is the key to true change. Denial, and minimizing will not help anyone. After we made it outside, she asked one last time "So are you really going to just throw away what we have like that?"

I responded back "You know what? We never had anything."

After that was said she went to her car and drove away, and I did the same. I continued my journey to Denver, and I thought about calling up another girl and inviting her to join me but decided against it. I just wanted to be alone at the moment and get my mind right. I had too much on my mind and didn't want to lose focus and make careless mistakes that would cost me.

When I arrived in Denver, I contemplated staying there for a few days to relax. I was mentally going over what took place at the apartment. I had mixed feelings of hurt, anger, and regret for how things transpired with Deidre. We got into it before, but it never reached that level. I wanted to reach out to her to apologize but was so embarrassed by how I acted. I didn't have the courage to call and face her.

While in the hotel room my phone started buzzing back to back repeatedly as if 10 different people were trying to call me at one time. I checked my phone and saw I had numerous messages and missed calls. I noticed one came from my mother and instantly got a nervous feeling in my soul. When my mom answered the phone, she was frantic and rapidly fired question after question without giving me the chance to respond before starting in on another question. "Boy, where are you? What have you and that woman gotten into? The police are looking for you, what the hell is going on?" I informed her I was out of state in Denver, CO, and asked her "Why are the police after me?" My mom told me that I was wanted for kidnapping, domestic violence with strangulation, assault with a firearm, possession of a firearm after a former conviction of a felony, and battery. She told me my face was all over the news, and that I better stay where I am until I can get this nightmare sorted out with a lawyer. At that moment I was thoroughly confused and shocked. I know we had our little confrontation at the apartment, but the charges that I was being accused of did not in any way illustrate anything close to the actual events that took place. At that moment all thought of being remorseful were out the window and were now replaced with pure hate. I would have accepted it if I were being charged with the crime that I actually committed. But she decided to flat out lie in order to get the desired result which will be me getting locked up, that's unacceptable. I quickly dialed out to my attorney to discuss how to swiftly take care of the nightmare that suddenly became my reality. I expressed to him my concern of the excessive and fabricated charges and the fact that I was on the news. He informed me the news coverage was "no big deal, all that means is those reporters had nothing better to report at that particular time" That did very little to subside my anxiety and worries about the situation I suddenly found myself in.

"So, what the hell do we do man? I can't withstand that sort of heat on my ass right now or ever! You can't just let her get away with those lies she reported!" I angrily stated.

"Whoa dude, you got to relax. I don't even know what evidence they have, and what they used to file the charges." "Haven't you been listening? There is no evidence because the whole damn thing is made up!" I almost screamed over the phone in frustration.

"Alright Oaks, I tell you what. When are you coming back to town?" The attorney inquired. I hesitated to tell him the truth as a sudden wave of paranoia seeped through my pores. "Uh, maybe next week." I stated.

"Ok fine, when you get back let me know and I'll arrange a walk through."

"Ok, that's fine, if at all possible, can you get these charges dropped yesterday? I swear to god they are false!" I pleaded.

"Ok we'll get it taken care of, stay in touch." With that the lawyer ended the call. I immediately called Deidre to confront her and try to record her on my phone admitting that she set me up.

"Hello?" she answered the phone with that attitude I've grown to despise.

"Hello my black ass! Why in the hell would you call the police on me and tell them a bunch of bullshit lies?" I seethed.

"Like what is wrong with you? I know we had a little conflict, but you know like I know, like god knows you made that shit up!"

I desperately hoped she was foolish enough to slip up and answer back truthfully, because I had the phone call recorded. Deidre responded simply

"You know what? You was just hollering that you was good on me, so I don't see the point of you calling me!" I almost lost all composure at this point.

"Are you out of your silly ass mind? This is not no damn game you fool!" I screeched. "You are playing with my life, and you of all people should know I can't take this now. With me being on probation in two different states, plus the weed charge I recently picked up." I was praying I could get her to slip and reveal her deceit on the phone.

"Look I have to go, I'm not available to talk to you right now." she told me snidely.

I couldn't believe she was really playing me like this. I instantly regretted not listening to both my mom and my dad when they warned me about dealing with that woman. I never saw anything in her character that would suggest we would ever end up in this sort of predicament. "Shit!" I yelled angrily and called my uncle Lil Rib for help. "What's up nephew? What do you got going on? I've heard about that bullshit with Deidre, man what the hell!" he questioned.

"Man Unk, I swear it's a bunch of fictional tales. She's playing some sick twisted game and I really don't even have the energy to talk about it now. I feel I'm going to be sick." I said exasperatedly.

"Please can I crash at your pad and lay low until my attorney clears this shit show up? You can't turn me down, I need you!" I begged giving him no room to shun me because of all the unwanted heat from the police.

"Alright it's cool come through, just be careful." I assured him that I would be. I packed and prepared to go back to Oklahoma to face the crisis head on.

I really would have preferred to stay in Colorado and deal with the charges from a safe, far distance. The problem was, my funds were low, all my money was invested in weed at that moment. All of my customers were in Oklahoma and they were ringing my phone nonstop. I had to go back to OKC so I could make all the money I can, as fast as I can because I knew I now had to pay for a bail and I would have to pay my lawyer, because of all the charges there were additional fees.

Once I made it back to OKC I hit all of my customers up and revealed my current location and told them to come and get what they needed ASAP because I'm going right back out of town in 5 hours, so no slow playing. I wanted to rush everyone along so that I can quickly hustle the funds I needed to take care of my immediate problems. Which would be lawyer and bail.

People were showing up as planned. I had 4 ounces in my pocket. One of my boys needed two and the other two were spoken for. I expected them both around the same time. The first guy pulled up, we handled business briskly and I'm sitting on my uncle's porch waiting on my other contact to show up. Out of nowhere all I hear is "Freeze! Oklahoma City Police! Don't move or I'll shoot your ass!" Despite that threatened command made by the officer, I foolishly tried to make a run for it. I was quickly tackled to the ground and handcuffed. Once the officers read my charges and Miranda rights, I was pat searched, and the officer confiscated the two ounces I had in my pocket. So now, you can add yet another weed charge to the growing list of felonies I now have to defend myself against.

I'm once again back in the OKC county jail, but this time my bond is $250,000. There's no way I can get that done so I have no choice but to focus on getting my lawyer paid. The rest of the weed I had was stashed at my uncle's house. I asked him if he can move it and put the money on my books. I sadly realized I'll be in jail for a while this time.

Due to the string of charges I had filed against me in Oklahoma, Kansas wanted to revoke my probation. They just kept setting my court date off to see what the outcome in Oklahoma will be first. This went on for nearly a year. In the course of that year, Deidre wrote me letters, put money on my books, and took over payments to the attorney. She repeatedly begged for me to forgive her for all this unnecessary drama that transpired. For the first six months I refused to say anything to her whatsoever. When I was going to court the District, Attorney offered me 20 years! I quickly decided that I don't want to take my chances putting up a fight when I know a sure way to end all this. I told Deidre that the only way we can move past this situation is for her to write a signed affidavit stating that she made those charges up and she will not cooperate in any way on any charge against me. She agreed and I had her make copies to send to the D.A, the judge, my lawyer, and myself. I was not going to be stubborn and literally take a 20-year gamble with my life. Once those letters were sent out, on my very next court date all my charges were dismissed except the possession of marijuana charge. My bond went from $250,000 to $50,000. My parents posted bail for me and I was finally able to be free again. I bonded out on July 3, 2017 and Kansas set a court date for August 17, 2017 1 month away. I didn't think too much of it because the serious offences that I was charged with were dismissed and the only remaining case was the weed possession. My lawyer had a deal worked out that was going to allow me to keep my freedom if I take and complete some drug classes.

So now, I am trying to slow things down tremendously. I've had entirely too many cases back to back over the same thing. I was worn out. Everything I thought I had quickly vanished and I'm back at ground zero. All I accomplished was making a big mess and the winning streak never lasted long.

I gained employment working at a moving company and at the Dollar Tree. It worked and I started to evaluate what to do with myself because the selling drugs, as my mama said, "Was just not meant for me to do." I went through a lot of the past two years going back and forth with various cases, so I just wanted to chill and try to figure out another route for me to pursue.

August 17, 2017 comes and it's my day to be seen at Sherman County Kansas Court. I was pretty confident that the case will get postponed because my next court date in OKC for the weed was at the end of August and I already had the deal for the drug class secured. So, when I went to the proceedings with my grandma. At the proceeding I was hit with the unexpected. The Probation Officer, District Attorney, and Judge sentenced me to seven years. I lost all the color to my face. When I first showed up to the courthouse, I overheard the Probation Officer tell one of his Colleagues ``I don't give a shit what he has to say we're maxing his ass out today." It wasn't good to hear, but I didn't fully believe the decision was solely up to him. I thought the judge would see that the cases I had against me were nonexistent and the only active case I had was still an open possession of marijuana case. I was wrong and in the matter of 5 minutes I was sentenced to serve seven years in the Kansas Department of Corrections for cases that were dismissed, and a weed possession case I was not convicted of.

I knew instantly that I was being railroaded. It made no logical sense for me to have to serve 7 years of my life in prison for cases that were dismissed. The alleged crimes weren't even filed in the state. My attorney in Kansas was outraged. Upon hearing the verdict, she barked "This is complete bullshit! I'm filing for an appeal immediately." She then looked at me and my now crying Grandmother and said she was so sorry. I asked her "Why am I doing seven years when I only had a 3-year probation term?" She explained to me in the State of Kansas that's how they do probation. If you complete it, you'll do less time. If you violate and get sent to prison the State has the option to make you do a little more than double of your original probation term. It flabbergasted me; I couldn't believe I am really being railroaded to a prison in a state I know nothing about for 7 freaking years! To make matters worse, I still have the open drug case in Oklahoma to worry about.

Three days after the sentencing, I was transported from the Sherman County Jail in Kansas and was taken to El Dorado, Kansas for diagnostics and processing. My mind was in a state of shock. It didn't feel real to me. Oftentimes I had the delusion that this was just some scared straight tactic, conspired by my probation officer.

I soon realized that this was no bluff. When I sat down with my case manager, she gave me my time sheet and my release date read June 17, 2024. I indeed was ordered to do 7 years by the courts. That will put me at age 31 at the time I just turned 24 the month before.

When I arrived at the prison Norton in North Kansas, I wondered why I was being housed at a high medium security facility. My official reason for being in prison was a "probation violation" no new felony convictions. I quickly sought out the case manager assigned to me and made inquiries about my security status. When the case manager looked me up on the computer, he printed some documents off and handed them to me. He explained I had 3 actives out of state warrants. One from GA, one from TX and the last one was from Oklahoma. The horrible news just would not stop coming in. When I was 18, I lived In GA and had a 10-year probation term for that state. I was in non-active status with that state for so long. I literally forgot the probation there still was valid. Texas was a misdemeanor warrant. I wasn't overly concerned about that one. My thinking was by the time I made it out of Kansas the statute of limitations will run out. The last active warrant issued was from Oklahoma. It was for missing the court date scheduled on August 25, 2017. In total between all three states I had 27 years on probation. All from marijuana related charges.

Day by day my soul was being turned into something dark and sinister. My mental state of mind was compromised. I could feel in my body I was dying. When I called home to speak to my dad and mama, they could hear it in my voice. My parents were so in tune they knew that something was dangerously wrong. My mama and dad decided to reach out to a lawyer to take action. It became obvious that I was being swallowed alive by the system, and something needed to be done. I thank god for my parents because they seriously saved my life.

Through the lawyer my parents retained, my GA warrant was dropped. That was a huge for me and gave me just the push I needed to start to fight back. I had been incarcerated for about 1 ½ and I've done nothing for myself because I gave up. With the GA victory I started to see the light at the end of the tunnel.

About every 3 months I received correspondence from my appellate attorney in regard to the appeal my attorney filed. Around the same time the GA warrant was dropped, the appeal was starting to pick up traction. With renewed hope, I decided to go ahead and get Oklahoma out of the way by filing a writ. A writ is basically legally forcing the state to either come and pick you up so you can face your charges in court or to dismiss your case if the extradition process is not executed in a certain amount of time.

Oklahoma came and picked me up from Kansas to finally bring me to court on the marijuana case. The previous offer on the table was to take drug classes and maintain my freedom. Giving the current circumstance I was in; my strategy was to accept a plea of 8 years in prison if they ran it concurrent with my Kansas time. In Oklahoma, a non-violent offender only does a fraction of their time so 8 years would only equate to 2 years behind bars. 8 years is the amount of time I had left on my probation so it would mean when I'm done doing time in Kansas, I will now be free of probation from every state. I already had almost 2 ½ to almost 3 years served in Kansas at that point. I communicated this strategy with my attorney and mother, both agreed this was the best course of action. The D.A accepted the offer and now my Kansas and Oklahoma time ran together.

I returned to Kansas and only after being back in Kansas custody for two months I received the most surprising news of my life. I won my appeal! The sentence was overturned, and immediate release court order was served. I was overjoyed and I couldn't believe the thought of going home was no longer a faraway fantasy, but now a foreseeable reality. Although I was ecstatic, it was a bittersweet moment because the fact is just two months ago, I signed for an 8-year sentence in Oklahoma, when I could have received drug classes. Unbeknown to me I would actually win my appeal. My strategy was to rid myself of all the probation time by doing all my Oklahoma probation time at the same time I was serving my Kansas time.

Instead of going home immediately, I now had to serve the remainder of my Oklahoma time. Since I received credit for time served, I expected to just process through Oklahoma diagnostics and within 3-5 months be released. Again, I was disappointed and had yet another obstacle. The way Oklahoma calculated their time is different than Kansas. Oklahoma calculates by the day. A 5-year sentence will equate to 2920 days. The time served I received was roughly 750 days. So, I now had 2170 days remaining to do! That's still around 2 years I would have to serve, so it's as if the time I've done in Kansas counted for absolutely nothing. I truly felt that I've walked The Long Road to Hell!

Brandon

The Long Road to Hell

This is an unconventional story of the person I used to be and how I arrived at my current situation, Hell. This story is probably unlike any other story you've ever heard but I am sure it is quite relatable to many.

In this chapter, I will give a brief history lesson on who I was, what I used to do and how I used to live. It is full of ups and downs, twists and turns and many unexpected events. The bottom line is this, it is all the TRUTH. So, lace up your hiking boots, pack your bags, and walk with me as I recount my terrible descent into Hell.

After I graduated high school, I had no clue what I was going to do. Naturally, considering all the drugs I was doing; I was destined for the streets. Partying, petty crime, couch surfing, I like to refer to it as the hippie lifestyle. During these times, I met a lot of important, loving people. A lot of them I've fallen out of contact with but still I wish them peace and prosperity. I like to consider myself a personable person and people tend to be attracted to my warmth. I feel like I used to take advantage of this quality and overstay my welcome. So, I bounced around in the streets a lot. Here for a month, there for two weeks, his house a few months, her house a few days. I've even slept under a bridge before. But this didn't deter me. I continued this lifestyle for years.

To make a little pocket money I stole cars, food, sold drugs, pan handled, worked fast food. None of these occupations were very prosperous and landed me in jail and stole my dignity. I partied and partied. Made acquaintances, stayed geeked up. I was really satisfied with the life I was leading but I knew eventually I would go to prison. It constantly loomed in the back of my mind. During one of my partying escapades I ran into an old high school buddy. And we became re-acquainted and began to kick it hard. For protective purposes we are just going to call him Shayde. Shayde was my guy. We would meet at different kickbacks, go our separate ways. Shayde was selling weed and would pull up on me when I had a swerve. Somehow, I used my personal ability and Shayde became my right-hand man.

This was sometime after the infamous Tulsa project X party. Me, Shayde, and another friend promoted one of the biggest, actually the biggest party I've ever been a part of. It was lit, but the venue wasn't suitable for the situation. We managed to bring out at least a couple hundred people to a 3-bedroom duplex. Cars lined the streets and people proceeded to turn up. The DJ was booming, there were plenty of beautiful girls, it was legit. I was doing my thing mingling with the party goers. Hitting beer bongs, smoking big blunts, freestyling and dancing. I watched people get sick and throw up. I watched people freak out on synthetic marijuana. Make out sessions. Man, it was wild!

Then the inevitable ensued. Pandemonium washed over the party like a tidal wave. It went from everybody enjoying themselves at one moment, to everybody fighting the next. I watched like 6 people get knocked out. Broken car windows, gun shots, knife wounds, it was definitely a project X party. At this time, I was living across the street in the adjacent duplex and was kicking it with the Marines (who partied hard) that provided the venue. I stayed and helped them clean up the place. It was a wreck, but we all had a good time. They ended up getting evicted, I ended up getting kicked out and the Marines let me crash with them at their new rent house.

More partying was unavoidable. Shayde pulled up, we partied. I ended up borrowing one of the Marines' Cadillacs one day without permission; drunk as fuck, wanting to show off for my friends and wrecked it. I didn't know what to tell him, so I didn't. I didn't return to their house until 3 weeks later. They were packing up and moving. No one was there so I left a note. It read along the lines of "Hey bro, I'm sorry about the car. I was drunk and joyriding and wrecked it. The police came and towed it. If I can help out in any way hit me up." Cowardly, maybe but I eventually recognized I was running away from the truth.

So, like the drifter I was, I found myself at another buddy's house. You can guess what we did, partied, got evicted. It was a pattern in my life. This was how I lived until I met Shayde. We linked up and one day while I was at his house, Shayde's dad told him to take me home and get his shit together. Shayde defended me and I remember his words to this day "you ready?" I replied, "Yeah let's do this shit." We left that night and didn't look back. That night we slept at the park, we were dead broke, and I can't remember for sure (probably from the drug use) but I'm pretty certain we slept in Shayde's car. We walked around and car hopped to find gas money and after that day, we were in full come up mode.

Now this was my first come-up where I learned I was a pretty decent hustler. For the longest time I was a consumer not the provider and with somebody to check the consumption we quickly bloomed. We were crashing with some people Shayde knew in a run-down apartment. The couple owned four or five dogs. One of them was recently acquired and this was the beautiful money maker. One day the dog lovers came to the conclusion that they had to find this new dog a home. They didn't have the space or food to maintain it. I saw the opportunity and hit it full speed like a starving great white who hasn't eaten for a month.

The dog was a beautiful 4-5-month-old, red-nosed pit-bull with honey colored eyes and a gentle demeanor. She was a sweetheart. I would've kept her if the circumstances permitted. But they didn't. And I was hungry literally and homeless. I proceeded to advertise the dog on Facebook, Craigslist, Twitter, and Instagram. We worded it nicely and made the dog appear incredibly attractive. The first potential customer drove from out of town to examine the dog. He apparently liked what he saw because he offered us $15 for her, which isn't much, but was $1,000 to my broke ass. I thought this was my big break, but I was quickly jolted out of my delusion. The lady dog lover did not like the idea of the man "bitching" the dog out. So, she denied him and sent us both away empty handed. I was infuriated and lashed out with harsh words at the woman and almost ruined our chance at selling the dog. Shayde quickly helped reel me back in and didn't allow me to blow the opportunity. So, our advertisements continued and after some denials, we found a suitable home for Honey.

A family answered our ad and told us that they had land and a good home and family structure for the dog and that's how we made our first $50 as a team. With that $50, we picked up an ounce of marijuana and began to network and sell it. We quickly sold out and re-upped. A friend I met in the county directed us to his cousin who was our supplier, and we climbed the ladder with urgency.

We were still drifting from here and there in order to save money. Sometimes we would rent a hotel for a few days and trap from there. With similar backgrounds and remarkably similar interests, you know we continued to party. At this point of my life I was satisfied. I always knew I was destined for bigger things, but this so-called "hippie" persona was in heaven. I feel like I was subconsciously running from my destiny and knew I had to correct it but didn't know how. One night at a little kickback, I was chilling with a few people, some I knew and some I didn't. I was enjoying myself jigging to the music, when this beautiful Native American with green eyes complimented me on my dancing skills. I said "thank you" or something of the like and continued to dance. After leaving I remember telling Shayde "I'm going to get her, watch." He replied back, we hopped in the car and drove off into the night/morning.

The next time I saw her, I approached the passenger seat of her home girls' car and noticed a dude in the back seat. I aggressively asked her "is that yo nigga?" she didn't answer so I repeated myself. She still didn't respond so I left it at that. We continued to kick it and this green-eyed Pocahontas eventually became a good friend. We crashed at her house sometimes and were in each other's immediate circle. Our relationship was completely platonic at this time and remained that way for a while. Shayde and I eventually found a plug with some California bud and even though he was taxing us we continued to come up. This would have to happen until we found something cheaper which was never to come considering the lifestyle we led. This lasted for a while and after a few different plugs, we found one that was worth our while. He had connections with the cartel, and the prices we were looking for. We formed a little team and trapped out of his apartment for a while.

We had this fake lean and sold it out of the apartment. The green-eyed girl said she had somebody to buy it. She pulled up with her friend and we waited for the clientele to arrive. He finally showed up. At this moment I was lit and slipping I admit. I had this idea that everything was running smooth until Shayde snatched me out of my revelry, Cheez, come on is what he said. I immediately snapped as the dude ran off with the product. We followed them down the stairs and one of them pulled out a gun. We were beat, we knew it, so we gave up the pursuit. The girl claimed she didn't know anything about it. But from that day forward I didn't know if I could trust the woman who would become the mother of my child.

Eventually we fell out with the plug we were staying with. I remember it like it was yesterday. One day we came up on some shrooms. We all ate some and watched Mac and Devin go to High School. After the movie went off, we smoked some more weed and kicked it. The plug must have started tripping and thinking we were out to get him. He was paranoid as hell, I'm pretty sure he was on meth. He called his homeboy. I kept a level head as the situation got heated. We packed our shit and eventually left. Not long after that I went to jail on a warrant for fines. It could have been much worse considering the illegal contraband we had in the car. I counted my blessings.

I did two weeks in the county when they let me out on a payment plan. I called Shayde and he picked me up from jail with some good news, he had a place we could stay. So, we pulled up to his baby momma's. Me, him, and the homie knuckles. Fresh out, we smoked a blunt and I got extremely high. One of our roommates, a beautiful petite brunette with a bubble butt walked out of her room with some booty shorts on and stood in front of us staring out the door. I was immediately attracted but my attraction was dwarfed by the homies. He sat there and started growling, literally. I lost it. I was so high, and he was growling a pelvic thrusting as she sat there and seduced us. She knew what she was doing and just continued to stare out the door. Meanwhile, I am laughing so hard that I am crying. I can't contain it. He was in his zone.

I eventually got settled in and we continued to sell weed. But with the house, this was the most stability we've had in some time. We settled down on the partying and drinking and just smoked a bunch of weed. Shayde's dad ended up becoming our plug and we finally had a steady supplier. So, we did this for a couple of months and eventually fell out, again. We all went our separate ways this time. Shayde took all the weed though and I didn't really try to stop him.

I ended up crashing at this appliance repair shop where a buddy from high school had a studio. We worked on an alarm while I worked part-time on washers and dryers learning how to repair them. This, like every other thing in my life, was short lived.

I remember the time where I decided I was going to make a change. Being small minded, it wasn't a big change, but it was major. The green-eyed girl and I became well acquainted. We were going steady for a while and she got pregnant. I stepped my hustle up into overdrive and she did as well and I eventually bought a car, fixed her car, and rented a house. I felt like I was finally growing up. I was, to a degree, but I remained a man-child years after.

Some life changing moments happened during the time leading up to me having my son. The first was the ultimate bad trip. Acid. Now that's a hell of a drug. One day I'm doing good, feeling good. I've been experimenting with acid for a little while now and I felt like it was time to up the dose. So, I call the homie. He wants some weed; I want some acid. We do a little haggling, and both leave the deal satisfied.

I'm trying to build a relationship with one of my girls' male friends and decide to invite him to do these tabs with me. He accepts my invitation and I proceed to start tripping. I popped two tabs before he arrived, and it hit me hard. I immediately felt bad vibes. By the time he got there, I was tripping.

I felt like the ultimate test of life was coming and I had to master my use of drugs at this moment in time. Long story short, I woke up in jail butt ass naked cuffed to a restraint chair without the slightest knowledge of how I got there. I eventually got my phone call and proceeded to call my woman. She recounted the events and my memory started to come back. It was ugly. Let's leave it at that. I bonded out and ended up getting probation.

After this acid trip, I was pretty much off the deep end. I've always been a spiritualist and I was enlightened to a new plane of existence and parallel universes and dimensions. It was crazy, I was crazy, and it was a mess. I became aware of this new power and sought it with vigor.

This had me looking completely insane. But I always kept a degree of logic on this pursuit of power. I realized I was a god and wanted to fully awaken my divinity. It was a long journey that eventually led me to hell. But if hell is where I needed to be, hell is where I'll go. I caught more charges, my probation got revoked and I went back to jail. This is where I first got acquainted with the vent. I was on a mental health evaluation pod in the county jail after fighting the police. I heard you could talk to the girls on the neighboring pod.

The rumor was confirmed when I hollered over there and got a response. I guess my vent was directly connected to their shower vent, at least that's what my first vent buddy told me. Her name still eludes me.

We would have conversations every once in a while, because it was probably awkward talking through the vent in the shower. After this incident I eventually went to prison for the first time after being on the run for months. And guess who set me up with the bondsman! You probably got it, my baby momma. Terrible. Yeah, I know. I don't blame her though, but she definitely played her part.

So, I was watching my son after not seeing him for months after me and his mother split. I remember talking to this girl who was liking my pictures on Facebook. Thinking with the head between my legs, I was trying to set up a little rendezvous. She had me intrigued. The next thing I know my baby momma calls me and says the bondsman is coming to your house. So, she picks me and my son up and I'm trying to get her to take me to her house so I could hide out. She tricked me like the cunning evil she is, and we went to a department store and I'm thinking everything is cool. Little do I know; the temperature is about to turn up. We're walking down an aisle and I see three men making a beeline directly towards me.

It took a moment to register, but when it did my instincts kicked in. I dashed off like a racehorse at the gates. They shot me with a Taser and after the acid trip, I was well acquainted with electricity, so I pulled it out and continued to run. I thought I had them beat when I climbed a ladder on another store, but they found me somehow. I climbed down the ladder. They had me surrounded. We had us a little Mexican standoff. They had a Taser, I had kung-Fu. I tried to hypnotize them with one of my forms and make a dash for it, but it didn't work. I did succeed in confusing them. I made one of the captors tase his colleague. We proceeded to wrestle on the ground where they tased me multiple times as I refused to cuff up.

Eventually I gave in and allowed them to secure the cuffs and I shouted obscenities at the devils who chased me down like a runaway slave. I laughed at the poor guy who got tased. I went to jail, then to prison. I knew I shouldn't have trusted that woman.

Chapter 2

Christopher

Poor Thoughts, Poor Choices

In Chapter 1 (The Long Road to Hell) I illustrated the sequence of events that led me to have a prison address. We will call that the "WHAT" now let's focus on "HOW" all came to be. This is an answer that my loved one's- Dad, Mom T, Mama, my sister Krystle, and the rest of my family that wants to know deserve to know. I too learned to find out the same thing. Why in the hell is this happening to me? I've pondered this question for years and came up with many different answers at different stages in my life. Let's start with all the wrong answers I've tried using to explain my circumstances.

As you see in chapter 1, I've had many run ins with the law. I've also caught the short end of the stick, on numerous occasions. I blamed society. I felt I was racially profiled and targeted. On four separate occasions the police were not truthful, or just in the tactics they used to put criminal charges against me. In Kansas, the Highway Trooper watched me cross the Colorado/Kansas border and immediately started following me. I had the car on cruise control doing 70 in a 75. When he pulled me over, I asked right away

"Why am I being stopped?" he replied to me

"You were speeding."

"Absolutely not! I was using my cruise control and I had it set for 70." I explained trying my best to mask my mixed emotions of anger and nervousness. I knew my fate was sealed when the officer told me this. "Well you know what? I smelled weed in this vehicle so I'm going to search your car! Where are you coming from anyway?" The officer had the nerve to ask me knowing damn well he's been following me ever since I crossed the state line. I never smoke in the vehicles I use to travel to Colorado in. He and I both knew he was lying through his teeth, but how could I have legally deflected his illegal search of my car.

When I was pulled over in OKC with my high school friend and the police found the weed in his possession, but because of his credentials of being in the military and mine being a convicted "drug dealer" I was unjustly charged with the weed. The money I had was legally possessed, but because of the bogus misdemeanor weed possession I now had two felonies: possession with intent, and possession of money proceeds. Two totally unnecessary and fraudulent charges.

The third encounter was the situation with Deidre. Even though I was in the wrong for the slap I gave her, all those other charges were unjustly filed. The only charge I should have had was either a simple domestic violence or an assault. You must have, to some degree, evidence to charge any person with a crime. How was it possible to be charged for possession of a firearm, pointing a fire, and kidnapping with not a shred of proof? I had no gun! I was in a whole other state when the complaint was made. How could I have kidnapped this woman? I now understand that the charges were purposely filed that way. The police knew from the start it was a flimsy, bogus allegation, but if they can stack the charges that way it will make my bond outrageously high and guarantee I can't make bail. I'm pretty sure this move was devised because she told them I sold drugs and they didn't want me to be able to bond out right away. Which would have happened if I was properly charged with the only crime I committed.

The fourth situation where I was failed by the justice system is when I went to Kansas on August 17, 2017 for my probation violation hearing and was sentenced to a 7-year prison term. The state presented zero evidence that a crime was committed by me to justify giving a maximum sentence. It was based on no convictions, and it was motivated by allegations that were dismissed. The appellate judge in Topeka, Kansas agreed and that was the reason why my sentence was overturned. It still cost 3 years of my life. At one point in time during my trials and tribulations I blamed god. I felt helpless and even though I know I wasn't perfect I felt I didn't deserve to be subjected to the things I've gone through. I looked back at the history of blacks in America and asked many times if I was just doomed from the start. When I really felt like God had no favor for me is when I was meeting child molesters, and rapists in prison doing less time than me. I could never understand how a sexual predator can do substantially less time than someone in prison for a "probation violation." Another wrong way that I was looking at the situation was minimizing what I've done. I always tried to justify selling weed by saying it's not a dangerous drug. It's a natural plant, it's not a serious crime. That may be my opinion but when it comes to going to jail, opinions are totally irrelevant. If it's illegal there's grounds for an arrest. Doesn't matter if it's identity theft or insurance fraud. If you don't want to go to prison don't break ANY laws. Those are all the wrong answers that I tried to believe in at one point or another during my incarceration.

Through growth and a deeper understanding of life, I no longer can blame my incarceration on the above circumstances alone. Even though I have legitimate reasons to be angry with the unjust and unfair system, I still cannot blame them fully on being the reason why I came to prison. I may have the opinion that a crime is not serious because in not hurting nobody, but it will still be invalid because when it comes to the law my opinions are totally irrelevant. My opinion on the seriousness of a crime and whether I believe my punishment should be minimal or not is the wrong type of mindset for me to have. Considering that I don't want to be incarcerated, I am not a legislator therefore I don't have control of the laws. There is a combination of several different elements that were contributing factors to my incarceration. The main reason is simply because I broke the law. There is no one else I can blame for this, absolutely no one. Even though things transpired the way they did, none of it would have ever even been possible had I not have left myself vulnerable to be railroaded. If I never would have been doing illegal things to begin with, there would have been no way I would have even been exposed to the risks. In order to have a chance to be a drafted in the NBA, you first have to at minimum be a basketball player. It is impossible to be drafted or to even have the slightest chance of being in the NBA if you never play. So, with that same concept, if you're not doing any type of criminal activity, you have zero chance of being drafted for the DOC (Department of Corrections).

My maturity level also played a major part in me being incarcerated. I was blessed to have great parents. They tried their best to raise me to be a successful, law abiding man of virtue. Growing up, I simply was not mature enough to take heed to the teachings of my parents. I was never fully comfortable with being myself. I came from a good family, but yet I wanted to fit in with the streets. Influenced by the hip-hop culture mixed with my ambition and lack of wisdom was the toxic combination that spelled trouble from the start. I was living life by my own understanding which was a fantasy world. My options for the success I wanted were limited.

51

Being a rapper, athlete, or hustler were the only three things in my mind. The first two were not panning out so when I tried the latter and had positive results, I became addicted. I was always told "when at first you don't succeed, try again." I misapplied that rule and used it were I shouldn't have.

My objective and intentions for writing this book is not to make excuses or justify anything I've done. I simply analyzed my life to the smallest of detail to try to get a clear understanding where I was going wrong and how to fix it. I realized how I was living was insane. Trying to repeatedly attempt the same thing expecting different results. Getting to this point in my life did not come about overnight. It didn't come about simply because I got locked up. It was a long, hard, and dark road I had in order to arrive at my current destination. Most people cannot understand what they don't see, so I'll attempt to give you a glimpse into my personal life experiences so we together can have a better understanding and hopefully do some good in the world. If this book can help even just one other person then my mission has been accomplished.

Brandon

Poor Thoughts, Poor Choices

Reading the previous chapter, you probably think I'm a leach, coward, and dumbass. Maybe not though, but reviewing my past is what I take from it. I was a leach because I always needed someone to be around, never doing anything on my own. I was a coward because I did everything possible to run away from my destiny. And a dumbass because it took me coming to prison twice to realize all of this.

Some may wonder what the cause of my stupidity was and upon self-examination, I found the direct source. Poor thoughts. Now it is only logic that poor thoughts lead to poor choices. Poor choices lead to poor actions. And poor actions lead to poor consequences. It doesn't take Einstein to figure this out. Looking deep inside, we will find the source of creating our reality. Our mind. Yep, my mind was in a bad place and continued to be until I figured out what was causing it.

Now, you may ask, "What were the poor thoughts you were thinking?" And I have an honest answer for you. I wasn't thinking and the thinking I was doing was ignorant, untruthful and vain. I thought I was this cool guy drug dealer that all the girls loved. I thought I was this super rapper that was going to make it and sign a major record deal. I thought I wasn't addicted to drugs and I thought eventually I would be successful entertaining these fabrications. Boy was I wrong! I was really a negative person though I always believed I was positive. This wasn't evident by the situation I found myself in life. All I reaped was negativity and wasn't man enough to accept that it was my fault. I was really indifferent to many situations and believed my destiny was to be a bum. So many things that bothered others wouldn't bother me.

I've always been a thinker though and aware of a higher power. So, though my thinking pattern was negative, I always searched for the truth. I had a destructive outlook on life, but I had a noble cause. With experience and wisdom, you will arrive at your destination. Fervently seeking, you are destined to find. And the truth is what I sought. I recently got there but we'll save that for later on in the book. Right now, we're talking about the poor thoughts that lead me to the penitentiary.

There are six major thought groups that constructed my current dilemma. Self-destructive, drug addiction and its denial, delusional thoughts, co-dependent thoughts, non-ambitious, and false egoistic thoughts. Let's start with the first, self-destruction. This is a terrible mind state to have especially when you are unaware of it. When you become aware of it you can correct it, but this is an arduous process and took me two trips to prison to figure it out. Being unaware of this mental condition you are stuck at a stand-still, continually ruining opportunities. You may have great potential, but you are scared, maybe even terrified of success. This was my case. I've had multiple opportunities and threw them away because of my xenophobia, the extreme fear of the unknown. I knew I had potential if only in one area of my life, but I didn't know the immediate road that led there, and this led to self-sabotage. A road heavily traveled.

One particular incident that I can recall happened as follows. I am an extraordinarily talented rapper/singer-songwriter and I've pursued music for years. One of my day one friends started producing for a local record label. Thinking of me and knowing my potential and talent, he set up a meeting to introduce me with his manager. Guess what I did preceding the meeting? I got sloppy drunk. I then proceeded to make a fool of myself. Yeah ignorant, I know. That's exactly what it was. Ignorance. I was unaware of what I was doing and therefore, continued in this negativity until I became hip.

The next thought group that led me to hell was drug addiction. I started smoking weed at 14. At 15, I was smoking more often and at 17 I was full blown pothead. I smoked weed every day. At school, before school and after school. That wasn't it. I started stealing cough syrup from the pharmacy and drinking whole bottles before going to school. No, this wasn't the fancy cough syrup the rappers' drink. It was, like I said, over the counter. I continued to use drugs after high school. And this drug use got worse and worse. I really didn't crave drugs, but I used them excessively. I feel like it was part of the image I was portraying and just something to do. So it wasn't that I was physically addicted. It was more of a psychological addiction.

As I said previously, it's all bad when you are unaware of your condition. I used marijuana, acid, shrooms, meth, opioids, prescription pills, the works. And continued to remain in a state of denial, using the mantra, "I'm a drug user, not a drug addict". Ignorant, I know but again that's exactly what it was. My ignorance thrived and dominated my life for the majority of my existence. Here on this particular walk. And not until recently, did I have the epiphany "Hey, you are a drug addict. Snap out of it dummy!" Seek and you shall find. And we sought relentlessly and eventually came to a conclusion, no matter how ugly it may have been.

Flowing down the list, next we arrive at the delusions. This set of thought was particularly treacherous. I stated I've always been pretty spiritual and was raised in a Christian household. While reading the gospel, I became fond of the lesson of faith. I took this lesson and ran with it. Now as I look back, I believe I ran the wrong way with it. I blew it out of proportion with the bible verse "with the faith of a mustard seed you can move a mountain". When I found myself in particular situations it worked. I kept my faith and God always saw me through. This is where I was mistaken though. It is said to have faith in God and to not put your trust in man. I kept my faith in God that he would deliver the perfect woman. My delusion was this one girl was the perfect woman and I just knew with my strong faith we would one day be together. This girl wrote to me a few times. The first time I was in prison and I was just sure we would get married and live happily ever after. Wrong again. I got out of prison, hit her up, liked a couple of Instagram pics and she told me she didn't want me to contact her anymore and blocked me. Dream of holy matrimony shattered. Yeah, woke my dumbass right up. I was heartbroken and didn't understand how I was going to continue to exist. Not because of this one event, but multiple events piled up. I was lost and distraught. I eventually had these revelations and continued to build my soon to be perfect castle, but it was a taxing task. Just like Rome wasn't built in a day, so neither is the realization of self-knowledge attained immediately.

Thus far we've gone over some detrimental thought patterns that I know many people fall victim to. I hope I am encouraging you to find your truth and live it. Next, codependency and being manipulated. From an awakened perspective, it seems atrocious to succumb to these thoughts and it truly is. I always believed I needed someone's help in order to succeed. I was a galaxy away from the truth. This is evident as I look in the rearview mirror and glance at my past. My mindset whether it be conscious, or subconscious was this: I need someone else to lean on in order to survive. For a long time, I was blind to my weaknesses. I had no idea what I was doing wrong, and how or why I kept   getting the results I was getting. It baffled me. And being codependent, my focus wasn't on the true source. I was blaming everyone else for my shortcomings. This was a counter-productive habit that eventually landed me in prison.

My first trip didn't reveal anything to me. I'm pretty sure that's why my second trip was inevitable. I was yet to learn my lesson. And finally sitting in the hole and hearing conversations through the vent, I found my problem and immediately began to correct it. I finally figured out the grim truth. I only have me and I must live up to my highest expectations. I can't let anyone make me the man I want to be. I have my own responsibilities to attend to like every other human being. So therefore, I must stand on my own two feet and pursue the man I intend to be.

Now in the same mindset, I noticed the fact that I allowed myself to be manipulated by people who wanted to use me for entertainment purposes. Weak-minded. Nothing more, nothing less. I have allowed multiple people to make a fool of me when I wasn't making a fool of myself. And I am the only person to blame. Whether it be to the childish choice I made early to do drugs and party like a rock star, or my seemingly nonchalant attitude towards life. I am the creator of my destiny and I reap what I sow. Understanding this, it is only necessary that I destroy this negative thought pattern and create a more productive one.

Just imagine having the potential of a king but being controlled like a pawn. In prison, they refer to it as being "juiced". This is when you allow somebody to hype you up or manipulate you to do something dumb just so they can laugh or use you in whatever way they deem necessary. This mindset is not in alignment with my greater self. I must embrace the true king within and begin to reign over my reality with proficiency and rely on my strengths and deny any other person the reigns to my life.

Now, we come to the non-ambitious thoughts. My whole life I lacked the drive to succeed, producing the bare minimum of what I needed to progress to a higher level. I believed I was destined for failure and I didn't have anything positive coming. I didn't want to work. I just wanted to kick it. But deep down there was a fire burning that just wouldn't tolerate being quenched. No matter how hard I tried to sabotage myself, the fire kept burning. Maybe it became just an ember at times, but it continued to glow. I tried, unconsciously, to just be content with the little to nothing I had but my truth wouldn't allow it. That flame was seeking tinder so it could stoke itself into the conflagration of the man I was to become.

With the destructive mindset of satisfaction, I continued to try and deny my flame any fuel. The lack of ambition. Maybe if I just sit here the flame will die out. Not so. We cannot hide who we are or continue to run from our truth. We will always have ourselves to deal with. Every time we look in the mirror one person stares back. Guess who? Yep, ourselves. And the only way to find your true self is through self-meditation. You must look on the inside to find what's causing your situation on the outside. Your outside circumstances are related to your inner mind state.

In my case, running from myself just got me closer to my destiny. And it was way more trying and taxing than if I would have accepted the fact; I'm lying to myself; this isn't my truth. I should be strengthening my weaknesses and using my strengths in order to succeed in my endeavors. This lack of ambition wasted many years of my life but ultimately came around full circle with an enlightening aura. Get off your ass, this isn't you. You are a predator in a world full of sheep. Unleash the wolf within and drive, eat, thrive.

The last mindset on the list wraps everything up and is the most detrimental of them all and the root which sprouted the tree of chaos. Not being true to ones' self. Man. It's a heavy topic and I've touched on it some in all the other categories. But let's look at it closer. Light conquers all. What is done in the dark will eventually be revealed. The truth will set you free. We have all heard these aphorisms and some may even say they're cliché, but in the grand scheme of things, truth prevails.

Scouring my past, I realized all the lies I've told to myself for self-gratifying purposes. I wanted to feed my ego these lies to justify my predicament and live in a false sense of security which made me feel safe. Playing these tricks on my mind, I created a mirage. I see this beautiful safe person but what's really there is an ugly, pretentious, self-absorbed monster, who is vulnerable and afraid of self-revelation. You want the truth? But you can't handle the truth! That was real for me. I wasn't ready for the truth.

I remember one crazy time during my experiments with drugs, I smoked some synthetic marijuana. As I got higher and higher, a voice entered my mind. This synthetic marijuana is known to make people hallucinate. In my case it was an audible hallucination. So, yeah, this voice entered my head and proceeded to tell me the ugly truth. It scared the hell out of me, and I began to panic. Just imagine you have this image you portray, and you've lied to yourself so much you truly believe it, then some random voice comes and undermines your whole existence. Tore me up. I started panicking and tried to control myself so I wouldn't lash out.

This self-revelation was so profound I didn't know how to perceive it. I remember walking around the house, repeating to myself "I need to calm down, I need to calm down" I calmed down and didn't heed the advice I was given and continued to prevaricate. This continued for some time and eventually landed me in prison. It truly is hard to take off the mask of deception and see the beautiful truth. Once you do, you'll never again want to put that mask back on.

For many people, the cause of this is wanting to fit and blend in. they don't want to reveal their truth because they're afraid of being judged as different. For me though, I've always been different. It was my greatness I was shirking away from. Terrified of becoming a true king, so I tried to rule a life of deception. It wasn't my destiny though, so I eventually shook off the disguise.

So, as you can see, these self-destructive thought patterns all coincide with each other. And once you find the root you will be able to stop that evil ugly tree from growing once and for all. Live your truth no matter what. Because if not, it will lead you into the worst situations in order to awaken you. Hence my example.

Chapter 3

Christopher

A Peek Behind the Fence

When you see movies like "Life" with Eddie Murphy and Martin Lawrence, or "Shaw Shank Redemption" with Morgan Freeman, you get a small glimpse of what a prison life is like. No matter how many movies or songs you hear about prison, they never seem able to fully capture the unique experience in every aspect.

Prison is, indeed, an entirely different world from the one we are accustomed to living. You might as well be on another planet, that's how foreign the environment is. When you first go to prison, you go to the diagnostics yard first. Every inmate goes there to be fully evaluated and documented. The officers want to know everything about you, from who your family is, to what gang you represent. You also go through a medical, dental, and educational examination. It seems that they try to gather as much information on you to create a profile. During the whole process you are dehumanized in every way. Your head is shaved bald, you are barked orders, you are subjected to strip searches where you get naked in front of the C.O.'s. They make you turn around, bend over, spread your buttocks, then cough. They do this to ensure you have no contraband hidden in your rectum. You're forced to shower in groups with other men. The food is laughable, borderline illegal and communications with your loved one's is non-existent. The entire process takes anywhere from 6-8 weeks. That is unless you piss off one of the guards at some point and they decide to push your file to the bottom of the list. There are no books. So, for the duration of your time there you are limited to only talking to your celly, working out, or sleeping your days away.

Once the process is complete and the DOC decides where to house you, they will call for you and load you up on a bus and transport you to the yard you will be doing your time at. Your legs and hands will be shackled tight and the long uncomfortable bus ride will last anywhere from 1 hour to 24 hours. Once you arrive at the prison you instantly feel the tension in the air. I remember when I got off the bus and walked on the yard with all of my belongings, I could see the stares and hear the inmates asking who I am and what gang I come from.

I held my head up high because I know better than to look like how I felt on the inside, which was nervous and unsure of my new surroundings. I got to my assigned cell and the only thing on my mind now is to get a hold of my family. I wanted them to put money on my canteen account so I can order food and hygiene. Before I do all of that, I had to take in my surroundings and get the lay of the land. After checking who my celly was and making sure

64

there was no immediate threat on the horizon, I then called my parents and my sister. I informed them that I am back in Oklahoma. I also broke the news to them that I will not be coming home as soon as we thought. I was frustrated and burnt out on being in prison. At that time, I had been gone for 3 years and it was weighing heavy on me.

Oklahoma now passed marijuana use as being legal and the state has dispensaries everywhere. This added to my frustrations because I felt I should've been released. My mentality was that I'm not here to make friends or to socialize, I just want to knock this time out as comfortable and quickly as possible. I'm not running in no gangs or I'm not answering to nobody. I quickly became an outsider because of my unpopular practices. It caused me trouble along the way because at the end of the day when you're alone, you're always the underdog in every situation.

The prison I was in had a lot of action going on. Meaning tobacco, drugs, and cell phones were available on the black market. I saw this as an opportunity to "do comfortable" time. My goal was to get a cellphone. The price of one was outrageous and I didn't want to bug my family for the money to get one. Instead, I did what put me in prison in the first place. I chose to hustle the money for one. I used $100.00 to get some tobacco and weed (I stayed away from the hard drugs). In no time, I had the phone, and it was worth the risk to me. The entire time I've been incarcerated, I haven't talked to my kids. I finally had a phone and was able to reach out to their mother's. I was also able to keep up with my family and friends on a daily basis. My mindset at the time was I should be home now anyways, so I'm doing time how I see fit. I stayed on the phone and did my time barricaded in my cell. I only dealt with other inmates when it came to business.

Prison being what it is, nothing good lasts forever. Especially when you're doing wrong, it all seems to come crashing down at some point. One day a group of inmates (about 3) decided they wanted to rob me for my phone. They passed as if they wanted to buy a canteen from me and got my guard down. Once in my cell, they jumped me and took my phone. I was irate at what just happened. I was bleeding and my eyes were swollen shut. I just lost in my mind my family. I couldn't/wouldn't accept that. I washed my face and went to the leader of their gang and told him what transpired, and I was willing to die over my shit. Politics being what they are in prison, if people are getting stabbed and war is breaking out, no one is making money and the police presence in the dorms will be heavy. No one wants that so to get to the bottom of the situation me and a few of my home boys demanded the phone back or we were stabbing the perpetrators on sight, no matter where that might be. Seeing that just because I'm not running in a gang, I will still stand up for myself. I earned respect in the shot caller's eyes and he made a deal that he would get my phone back if I fought for it.

I accepted the condition, and I fought the three people who robbed me. I was already in bad shape from being jumped not even 30 minutes prior but to get my phone back I paid no attention to my condition and fought anyway. In prison once your reputation is tarnished and you're looked upon as prey. You will be preyed upon repeatedly. I was not willing to allow this to happen. I went multiple rounds with each of the inmates and I got my phone back as promised in spite of my eyes being swollen shut, lip being busted up, and body being sore, I still felt happy to get my phone back and others didn't. They looked at it like the shot caller sided with me instead of his own gang. It was said that because I was alone, they should have been able to jump me, take my phone and get away with it. There would be no repercussions many thought they were cowards to try to pick on someone because he chose to move alone. Instead of taking a phone from a rival gang member why pick on the loner?

There were many different opinions about what took place and the very next day I was robbed and beat up again! A member from the same gang, but who was housed on another compound came to my cell while I was asleep and started punching me in my sleep. Once again, my phone was lost, and I was now beaten so badly that I was unrecognizable. I couldn't believe what just happened. I'm thinking "what did I do to deserve this?" no one gave me anything. I grinded for what I had. Why am I going through this shit? Something inside of me snapped. I knew then and there that at that moment, that I'm put in a certain situation and my back was against the wall, I will kill. I got a knife and put it in my boxers and walked outside my cell. People saw me in my bloody clothes and wanted to know what happened. Word circulated quickly that I was robbed again. This time, things were different. A few people that I was cool with came to me and said "Enough! I'm riding with you." I will never forget my boys Renegade, Cudy, 5'7 Rob, Dmessy and Julio. They came to me and let me know that whatever I wanted to do we're going to do together. No matter what, there will always be people to ride behind a righteous cause.

The plan for me was simple. I'm getting my phone back, and I'm making a statement to everybody on the compound, "I will not be bullied and preyed on!" So the people who aligned themselves with me, sent word to the individual who beat me up in my sleep and took my phone that he has exactly 24 hours to turn the phone over or it's going to fall. That day I did something that I never in my life thought I would ever do. I was not in my right state of mind and never been in a situation like this before. My boy Renegade is doing a 75-year sentence for a homicide committed while behind bars. He explained to me how war goes on in prison and how to increase my chances of survival. He pulled a bag of meth and started snorting some. He explained to me that Hitler's Nazi army created meth as a drug to produce "Super Soldiers." You lose your desire to sleep, you have no feelings of pain and you lose your cognitive thinking skills giving you the ability to do anything that's necessary for battle without hesitation. Hesitation and being caught slipping off guard are mistakes resulting in death. Convinced of his logic I too indulged and snorted meth for the first time.

What we were planning to do was similar to a suicide mission. We were six deep taking on a gang of one hundred plus members in that yard. We were definitely taking a page out of the movie "300." When the 300 Spartans bravely went against the multi thousand-man persuasion army. When I got high the pain, I had from my injuries were non-existent. My mind was in war mode 100%, and I was energized tremendously ready to take on whoever, whatever and wherever. We waited to get word back on whether the phone will be returned. As expected, the warning was not being taken seriously and it was obvious, I would have to follow through on what I knew all along I would end up doing. We waited until the right time and snuck to his cell. Since we were outnumbered by a landslide the best course of attack was the element of surprise. What worked to my advantage was the arrogance of the fool who took my phone. Thinking there would be no retaliation, he was comfortably in his cell with two of his homeboys laid back playing on my phone. I gave a cigarette to a random inmate who knew of nothing I was planning and told him to knock on the guy's cell. "When he answers, you just get the hell out of my way!" I instructed. He did as I asked of him and when the door was answered, me and my five-man army barged into the guy's cell. When he saw my face, he tried to say something. I didn't give him a chance to utter a single word. I swung my knife and stabbed him several times. With no regard to where I was aiming, my only goal was to draw blood.

As I could barely see out of my eyes, he screamed and fell to the floor in obvious pain and turmoil. I covered his mouth with one hand holding the knife to his neck with the other and said "I'm only saying this once. Where's my phone?" He pointed to his bunk and one of my homeboys went to get it. The two homeboys that were in the cell with the person who robbed me were being held at knife point by the allies who came with me. The looks on both of their faces was of pure terror. I recalled seeing all three of those inmates running around the yard with their chests puffed out and with much bravado. I saw none of the head gangster exterior that they were always portraying at that moment in that cell. I remember loving that feeling.

We retrieved the phone and made our way back to our side of the compound when we got back, we immediately went to hide out in my boy Renegade's cell. Once there, we listened to music on the loudspeakers he had in his cell, we did more lines of the meth and celebrated the small victory we had. We were expecting an anticipated retaliation therefore, no one was going to sleep anytime soon, and we agreed to always be around each other. No one will get caught by themselves.

While we were in Renegade's chilling and listening to music, knives at close distances ready for whatever, an associate came to the door and told us it is falling down right now between the Bloods and Hoovers on the pad. Curious as to what was going on and the fact that the issues I've been having was with the Hoovers. My mixed group of rebellions decided to go and see what was going on. Never wanting to be in the blind on things because that's how you get caught slipping, we played the background and watched the chaos from a distance.

From the bits and pieces of conversation I heard from one of the Hoovers, we discovered a phone was taken from a Hoover by some Bloods who went to his cell and robbed him at knife point. It seemed to me like a major coincidence of the timing that they decided to make a move on J.R.'s phone. Smooth and Moe were the bloods that did the robbery, and their reasoning was because they heard J.R. used to want to be a blood then switched over to be a Hoover. That logic didn't make sense to me being that we've all been on this yard together for several months now and J.R. been had a phone and now all of a sudden, this issue arises.

The Bloods and the Hoovers arrange several one on one fights between the two gangs so they can squash that beef and move on. Moe and J.R. fought for J.R.'s phone and J.R. lost it. After around six to seven different one on one sessions the gangs called a quits because the police were starting to get restless. They allow violence to go on knowing it's impossible to stop, but only to a certain extent. They would much rather us fight than people getting stabbed and killed.

Later on, that same night, Moe and Smooth came to my hangout which is Renegade's cell and they asked to holler at me. Skeptical but curious, I let them in and we all quiet down to listen to what they had to say. Moe pulls out some Newport's and offers me one and lights one of his own. I cautiously take the cigarette half expecting a trick or an ambush of some kind. Moe than looked at me and said, "You know why that shit went down today?" Even though I had a clue I remained silent and waited on him to explain himself. "We've been watching you these last few days and we know what you've been going through. We didn't like it, so we looked you up to see if you were a sex offender or a snitch to try to figure why you were being targeted. You came out clean, so we knew they were just trying to prey on you because you're by yourself and that's sucker shit! Why not oppose a rival gang? So, if they want to get on some bully shit, we can too but we'll go for the opps not a civilian." I figured that's what their motivation was but didn't have confirmation until then. "Besides, you stood up for yourself and went hard so we respect it." Smooth added. We smoked the cigarettes together then they left the cell.

Once me and my boys were alone, we speculated what the next move will be. "Now that the Bloods made their move the Hoovers won't retaliate. They're not dumb they know the real reason why it went down today." Dmessy stated. "Yeah, well just in case everything stays the same, no one gets caught alone and we keep the knives in arms reach." Julio added and we all agreed.

Two days later our entire unit was on lockdown. The C.O.'s we're going cell to cell shaking everyone down. Most likely it was brought on by all of the violence that transpired the past week. When the police came to my cell, they found my hiding spot for my phone and took it. I was devastated, after everything I went through for that damn phone just to lose it to the police not even a full 48 hours later. I was placed in segregation housing for a few months. While back there I reflected on past events and came to the conclusion none of it was worth it. I took a chance with my life over something that was petty. I told myself when I get out, I'll just chill and focus on going home. I can have a phone when I get out of prison!

When I got released from lockup, my homeboys were there to welcome me back. Renegade had some meth and offered me some. I declined and told him "I'll never mess with that shit again." I did accept the weed that was passed to me though. They showed me a song that Nico and Klow made using a studio app on the cell phone since I been on lockup. They had given us all a shout out from the war we won against all odds. We laughed and reminisced of those crazy times and how we all came together. Cudy and Renegade told me they had a surprise. I asked what it was, and they produced a large bag of tobacco. "Yo, ever since we went against the Hoovers the Ese's have been plugging us in with the tobacco for cheap." said Cuddy proudly. Renegade tossed the tobacco to me and told me "that's all you, shit you'll have another phone in no time." I was shocked by the amount of tobacco he gave me. I would be able to buy another phone and still have some extra. The thoughts I had in the hole about not getting another phone soon vanished from my mind and my new goal was to hustle up another phone. I rationalized that it was free and didn't have to come from my family's pockets, so it'll be ok.

Within three weeks I had another phone and was back in business. Everything was going well for a short period, then out of nowhere all hell breaks loose. An inmate was badly stabbed and had to get medically flown to the hospital where he later died. That put so much heat on the dorm all of the C.O.'s and administration conducted a massive shakedown. Ever since the drama, I was involved in a transpired a few months; I always felt the need to keep a blade on me at all times. Even when I slept. At the time I didn't realize how serious the incident was involving the inmate that was attacked. I was stopped by many officers walking on the compound and randomly searched. I was caught with two knives and my cell phone. Immediately I was taken to the hole again. This time was different than before. I stayed in Seg for an unusually longtime, with no word of a hearing. I should have had a hearing within 10 days of being in the hole. After several months, the Chief of Security came to my cell and had me escorted to his office.

Once we got there, he began asking me "So what gang are you running with? Why are the Hoovers interested in you?" I told him "I'm not in a gang and if anyone is after me, I'm not sure why." "Oh, so you're going to play it like that? I never ask a question I already know the answer to son." he says to me watching my every movement.

"Really man, I'm not in a gang. It is possible to be black and not be gang affiliated?" I said to the Chief, irritated that he keeps trying to push the gang affiliation on me.

"Stand up and take off your shirt son." the Chief commanded. I did as I was told and took my shirt off, exposing all of my tattoos. The Chief and two of his C.O.'s began taking pictures of my tattoos and documenting them. "Alright, well there's been a lot of shit going on around here and when I dig into it your name surfaces on more than one occasion. Being that I don't like shit on my yard, especially when it puts heat on me. I'm going to purge any and every nuisance that is brought before me." As the Chief told me this, I processed to believe the fact that someone is telling on me. "All of those wanna be tough ass gangsters and someone feels the need to tell the police on me?" I'm thinking to myself. It was a surprise to me considering the fact I wasn't the aggressor. I was provoked and attacked first and acted only in self-defense. "We're done here." the Chief told me, snapping me out of my thoughts.

When I was led back into segregation, I saw all of my boys that I've grown to call "friends" in different cells. We were all getting shipped in different directions. They were also caught with knives and phones. I was transferred to another medium security prison. It is a private prison run by an organization called Cimarron. All movements here are controlled far different than the open state yard I just came from. We are locked down most of the time.

When I first arrived at Cushing (that's what the nickname for the yard is) I was placed on a regular pad. I stuck to myself and opted not to get involved with nothing I shouldn't have. I evaluated how things went in Lexington (my previous yard) and considered myself lucky I only walked away with a transfer. I had many unnecessary close calls and at this point my only focus is to go home.

My strategy was to keep to myself and not get involved with nobody. I have 2 years left to do and I planned on doing the remainder of my time as a loner. This always seemed to get me into some sort of trouble. The reason being that I am too young to not be running around with a larger group. The only ones who can play lone ranger and not be bothered are old school inmates. They can do their own time and not be bothered. When a young person is seen to be a loner or outcast, it makes him a target because it looks as if something is wrong with him whether it involves being a sex offender or being a "snitch". Neither is good to be identified by and can lead to being targeted.

I refused to conform to typical prison life by running around with gangs or falling into prison politics. I believe in being my own man and answering to no one but myself. That and being tired of being in prison in general, feeling like I should already be home. I was very standoffish. I intentionally gave off the vibe that "I'm not here to make friends and I don't want to be bothered." Hoping people would take the hint and leave me alone. This of course did not happen, and I soon found myself being confronted by another prison bully.

It was canteen day and I just ordered my food. I'm standing in front of my cell waiting on the C.O. to let me in and I'm approached by an inmate called "Grave-yard." He saw that I had a few boxes of Duncan doughnuts, Debbie cakes and he asked me for them. I can tell by the way he asked me, he was trying to punk me out of my food. I never had any conversations with him or never had any dealings with him. I found it odd he would all of a sudden come up to me and ask me for my stuff. I told him no and out of nowhere he blind sides me and hit me in my mouth in the middle of the pod in front of everybody. My mouth was split wide open and I had to get 10 stitches to seal the open wound. Since it was done in front of the C.O.'s he was immediately taken to the "Phase Program". That is long term segregation where they hold you in the hole at a minimum of a year. There are strict guidelines to follow if they are not you will stay in the program as long as it takes until completed.

That same weekend I had an unexpected visit from my sister Krystle, Aunt Shonnie, Uncle Brandon and my Mama. When I first walked into the visiting room my family saw me from a distance, they were all smiling and waving excitedly as I walked over to them. The closer I got towards them; I saw the look on all of their faces when they saw my busted stitched up lip. The look of hurt and concern in their faces shook me to my core. I saw the fear they had in their eyes for me and it made me feel bad because no matter what I say, I know I won't be able to erase the worry that they will have for me. The last thing my mom told me before the visitation ended "Son, you be careful, and you come home." That did something to me. It made me feel my mom was afraid for my life. I wish I could have made her feel sure that I was ok, but I couldn't. My sister and mother informed me that recently an inmate used a cell phone to reach out to my sister Krystle on Facebook and threatened my life. Even though the threat was idlily made and impossible to be carried out, between that and the incident that just took place made it impossible to settle my family's anxiety.

I took it hard and personal because of some ignorant fools in prison trying to intimidate and be bullies. It's causing my family stress and pain. I think it caused more pain for them than myself, because I am here, I can evaluate a serious threat versus one that is insignificant. My family has no way of knowing the seriousness of various situations, therefore it will cause them to panic and worry all the time. I couldn't stand the thought of someone else compromising my family's peace of mind. From that moment I decided anyone who puts my safety in jeopardy or wants to cause me harm, I'm taking it to the extreme every time. I will not fight anymore, if anyone wanted to bring violence my way, I'm handling it with a knife.

I saw the results I had the first time I used it and liked the feeling of security and power I had. I felt protected and safe. No one wants to die by being stabbed. If people know you are willing to take things to that level, then they will most likely go and find a weaker and easier target. I made a prison knife at the prison I was at before. I went everywhere with it. I was prepared to make an example out of the very next person who tries to bring harm my way. I don't bother nobody. I stay to myself and therefore have every right to be left alone.

In my mind I already figured I would work the self-defense angle using the fact I was assaulted before for no reason and I am not a gang member. Therefore, I am extremely outnumbered, and I was in fear for my life. With that in my mind I was fully prepared to use it if I needed to, feeling I had a good chance to get away with it, because I was assaulted and my lips busted open in front of everybody. I was afraid that would encourage future attacks from other inmates. They would have looked at my attack as a sign of weakness and just like sharks being attracted and lured in by blood, inmates are attracted and lured to weaken inmates.

For the next few weeks nothing really transpired, but like the calm before the storm, I felt it would only be a matter of time before drama came my way. For this reason, I refused to get caught anywhere without it. I could tell by the way the inmates on my pod talked about me that they thought I was lame and weak. Not knowing everything I just went through and overcame at the last prison I was in. All they saw was me getting punched on and not doing anything back. Before I ever had the chance to be antagonized, I was caught with my knife by the C.O. I was coming out of my cell to walk to chow hall for lunch when the knife fell through a hole I had in my jacket. The knife fell on the floor right by the C.O.'s boot. I tried to recover it as quickly as possible and hide it in my pants. "What was that?" questioned the guard. "Nothing man, it was just my pen." I replied to the guard pulling a pen I had from my pockets. "No way, give it to me now!" the C.O. commanded and at the same time calling over the radio "inmate has a knife!" I panicked, not wanting to get caught with the weapon red handed. I pushed passed the guard bursting into the nearest open cell to me and flushed it down the toilet. The guard was in a panic and tried to lock me in my neighbor's cell. I too was in a panic and didn't want him locking me in someone else's cell, so I pushed against the door and barged past the guard, causing him to lose his balance and fall.

When the C.O.'s back up arrived, he was picking himself up off the ground. This gave the other guards the perception that I was fighting with the pod officer. All they hear is a "inmate has a knife", in a hysterical voice and when they come on to the pod their coworker is picking himself up from the floor. This puts the rest of the guards on full alert. "Freeze!" they shouted to me in unison. "Get the fuck on the ground!" the LT on the shift yells pointing a laser sighted pepper spray pellet gun in my face. I immediately complied to their commands and got on the floor to be cuffed up. I am then taken to the segregation unit and placed in the hole.

I'm in the hole for a few weeks on "pending investigation status" when the Chief of Security comes to my cell to have a word with me. "Why didn't you just give it up?" he asked me. "Give up what? I only had a pen. The C.O. thought he saw something else and panicked." I lied trying to keep in my mind the knife was never recovered, therefore they can't prove I had a weapon. "Oh, you want to try to play that game with me huh?" the Chief sneered. "Well if that's the story you're going with, you'll go from getting a write up and phase time to having a free-world case put on you for assault on an officer." I quickly realized I was in a lose lose situation. Although they technically can't make the weapons charge stick, he is forcing me to admit ownership of it or he'll file bogus assault charges against me for pushing past the door when the C.O. tried to lock me in my neighbor's cell causing him to fall. Although it would be a weak case, it would stick because that slight contact is all that's needed to make an assault claim. The last thing I needed was to have a free-world case filed against me. I reluctantly admitted to having the weapon. I tried to level with the Chief and explain everything I've been through and that I meant no harm. I just felt unsafe and needed it for protection.

"Although I can understand your dilemma, I still have a job to do and can't let this slide." The Chief of Security informed me. "I'll just drop the assault allegations and we'll just deal with the weapons infraction." he negotiated with me. "That's fair enough." I admitted. Then the Chief left my cell. After I was found guilty at my discipline hearing, I was sentenced to do a phase program (long term segregation).

Brandon

A Peek Behind the Fence

Wonder what I've seen in prison? Here is a brief glimpse. After leaving Sevyn, the red-haired girl I grew to love over the vent in the County, I arrived at Lexington A&R. A four-hour trip from County jail, led me to my dreaded destination, the pen. Being the second time in two years, I already knew what to expect; Baloney sandwiches, my whole head and face shaved bald, signing my will, a prison rape video, and getting butt naked and getting my tattoos recorded. All of these things are humiliating and designed to frighten you. And for a lot of people it works as planned.

For me, though, I used to carry an attitude like "it is what it is" So I wasn't necessarily scared, I was more accepting of my situation and prepared to deal with the outcome. And after a long 24-hour day with no sleep I arrived at my cell.

Immediately, people started gang banging showing their sets dissing other people's sets. Pandemonium. Being a gang member, or at least trying to be, I proceeded to indulge in the turmoil. I specifically recall getting into it with this one guy. He dissed my set, I dissed his. We came to the conclusion that we were going to fight once the chance presented itself. It never came. He came to my cell before he left and tried to drop some wisdom on me, though he was a few years younger. He said, "bro this gang banging shit is watered down, nigga's snitching and some more shit just do you." It was a truth that I continue to battle for a long time. Eventually this person came back to my cell at a different facility. I didn't recognize him, but he recognized me. Working on myself, I allowed him to come in, though he was from a different set because he mentioned he only had 10 days to go. Long story short we felt the flu together and shared ideas and beliefs, then he discharged. He just wrote me with some good news. And hopefully we stay acquainted. Teamwork makes the dream work baby!

Before I left A&R the yard went on lockdown. It was reported that Bloods fell out with the natives. And me being a blood, I was preparing myself for war. And guess what? I just happened to land at the same yard I just fell down at. My luck. I proceeded to get accustomed to the prison life and this 15 year stay I had in front of me.

Understand, I'm still having side effects from the terrible acid trip that messed up my head. So, when I smoke weed, I just go into another dimension. At least that's what I call it and enjoy my interdimensional high. Yeah sounds crazy right but it gets worse. I will walk around the pod barefoot singing loud and doing Kung Fu. I was a mess. I was the crazy guy on the pod. But I really wasn't as crazy as I was pretending to be, I just adopted this attitude to truly not give a care and search the depths of the universe. Why not embrace my crazy? I have 15 years. This was my attitude until the rude awakening.

Being this weird dude that was anxious and loud I was bound to get in a fight. And fight I did. On one occasion, I just had a feeling in my gut somebody was talking about me. I went to the belief source of the problem ah my gut was right. There were three bloods talking about me. We proceeded to fight, and I use some of my makeshift Kung Fu to defend myself. They threw blows. I evaded. Through some blows of my own, I eventually fought my way out of the sale. After getting out of the sale they didn't want to fight anymore. I wanted to give the pod a show. I stormed off and the guy I kicked it with offered me a knife and was ready to ride with me against my assailants. We proceeded to push into battle but were stopped short of the battlefield. Another homie ended up talking me out of doing my little mission. Thank God because there is no telling what I could have done or where I could have been now. Divine intervention? Just maybe.

I continue to have problems gang banging and using drugs. My business was always good, so nothing ensued from me owing anybody, but I definitely have more squabbles. On another occasion, I'm outside enjoying recreation time, high, walking around in the mud. I was basically like this hippie thug trapped in a world of lies, ignorance and confusion. Another homeboy comments it a smart remark. Something along the lines of "those days are long gone or something Implying I was doing some caveman dance. I got mad, called him out and we got down. We went to a designating fighting cell and went blow for blow. There was a homie from his set and one from mine. They looked confused because as we squared away and tried to punch each other lights out, I laughed maniacally. They thought I was a madman, boy, only if they knew. We continued to swing on each other until he landed a blow that chipped my tooth. Once I noticed it was broken, I called the fight to a stop. We shook hands and I walked back to my cell where I nursed my wounds.

My celly at the time was a good dude. Another blessing of many I squandered away. I did drugs and lived like a true bum. And he continued to accept me and helped me throughout our living together. I eventually had a fight with him as well. With all these fights I didn't understand the truth there I was fighting myself it's not them it's me. This revelation was destined to reveal itself sooner or later and after my last fight it finally did. We'll get there though.

After I moved out of the sale with the best celly I could have, because of my ignorance, I moved in with a fellow drug addict. Now this guy was a character, as was I. But I spent my money on drugs; he made his drugs by being a source of entertainment. The dude literally had two dicks tattooed for his eyebrows. Crazy? Tell me about it. You can get a glimpse of where my mind was. I was just going to stay high and live that life of a prison junkie and do my time. Meanwhile, my true self was dying to come out. I continued to try to smother him away.

At this yard I was at there were beautiful nurses, case managers, and doctors. It was really the best place I could have been, but I am notorious for sabotaging my own opportunities. On many occasions I was flirting with staff and had inmates tell me. I was eccentric, still am, so I guess I was mysteriously attractive. Probably not though. I continue to believe this delusion. But I can't lie, the ladies were giving me play and instead of capitalizing, once again I threw away beautiful opportunities. I met some of the most beautiful professionals in prison. Becoming aware of their existence is one of the reasons driving me to complete this book as we speak.

I noticed a couple of these beautiful women at the annual talent show. I was supposed to sing this Islamic song with a buddy but reneged because I wasn't really Islamic, and I didn't want to portray myself as such. So, I declined. But later on, that day as I was in my own world meditating on nature and her beautiful ways, playing in the rain, I heard some music. I am irresistibly drawn to the melodious vibrations, so I followed them. They led me to the talent show. Everybody knows me on the yard for dancing. That's what I do when there's music around. And I'm pretty good. So, I made it to the talent show fashionably late and just vibed to the music while another group performed. It was dead, completely. Nobody was cheering until they noticed me in the background doing my thing. They encouraged me to go to the front stage and I did. I made my grand appearance and proceeded to steal the show. It went from silence to the crowd going crazy. I finished my freestyle routine with a funky ass air guitar solo. I killed it. Or so I thought. Everybody knew me around the yard after that, but my decline continued. I went through the ringer man. Really, I put myself through the ringer. I continue to succumb to the delusions I was having and not strong enough to throw them away and be realistic.

The drugs played a major role in my outlook on life. And in prison, contrary to some people's belief, they are prevalent. I stayed high in prison all the way up to the trip to the hole from where I'm currently writing to you. And yeah there are still drugs back here. It's an everyday battle to keep a positive mind and stay away from the negativity especially in my current predicament.

While I've been in prison, I've ran into every drug that's out there on the streets. Weed, Meth, Heroin, Xanax, Oxy, you name it they've got it. People may think all prisoners are stupid people who've been caught doing something illegal. This may be true to some extent, but I've witnessed some pretty crafty maneuvers to get drugs and phones into the tightest facilities. Its mind blowing what some people will do and are willing to risk for some money or a high. I've seen people keister phones, drugs, knives and all. Where there's a will there's a way, I guess. But me, I never got into all the complicated intricacies of being a penitentiary dope boy. I was just a consumer. My drug of choice was Mary Jane, but on a few occasions, I've bought some meth. Yeah, the horrible, horrible taboo. I must admit, meth to some people, turns them into the worst person you can imagine. But for me it was an occasional thing, and I didn't ever let it get control of me.

The prison system is full of scumbags and the lowlifes of society though. There is a concentration of liars, killers, thieves, and drug addicts. Which makes it hard to do the right thing. The court system gives you an excessive amount of time for a minor problem without truly reviewing your case or history and expects you to correct yourself in the presence of all of the wickedness.

My wild, don't give a hoot manner eventually led me to segregation where I began recreating myself. I went to the hole this time because someone, again, told on me for trying to "Mack" on an employee. After all this chaos I knew I had to become a different person and leave my old ways behind. I was so far gone; this wasn't an easy task and the struggle still continues today.

I began searching my inner depths as I sat in segregation. I meditated, medicated, and elevated. I was notified that I would be shipping to another yard. I decided at this new yard I would start fresh. New name, no more gang banging and hustling. I sat in there and shot the breeze with my celly and other inmates that were connected to my vent. I tried to plan my future moves but they weren't thorough and consequently they failed.

During transport I happened to get into another altercation with a rival gang member. Our hands were cuffed to our waist and we were shackled. We exchanged obscenities and different threats to each other. We had a standoff and eventually I proceeded to headbutt him and knock his tooth out the only thing possible to do considering my hands being cuffed. I just couldn't give it up. I continue to live in this altered consciousness. The thing is I knew I was messed up but didn't know how to change. A problem I'm sure a lot of prisoners' faces. But instead of putting us in a positive rehabilitative environment we are locked in a small, compressed warzone where at any second you can lose your life. So, it's either eat or be eaten. At least that's what I thought. I ended up getting put in the single cell on the bus for the rest of my ride for my little display of rebellion.

During the remainder of the trip I built up anxiety, knowing I want to change and knowing how hard the fight is. And I know arriving at a new facility, more battles lurked ahead. The bus finally stopped at my current location. And I readied myself to implement my busted plan that not to my surprise failed miserably. I continue to clean to the past and didn't want to let go, but I knew I had to if I wanted to turn around my current predicament.

I ended up settling in. The first celly I moved in with was filthy and a drug user. We didn't last very long. After I found a carton of spoiled milk under his bed, I called it quits. I had enough.

After him I moved in with the Muslim who at first seemed intelligent, refined an active. But like the cliche goes; Looks can be deceiving. And deceiving they were. Not long after I moved in, I realized it was a big mistake. Yeah, I'm weird but I'm constantly evolving in trying to become the best man I can be. This is damn near impossible living with the 27-year-old child. We ended up fighting long and hard and then having a long hard talk afterwards. I thought this would change things, but deep down knew differently. A few days later he fell back into his old habits. He was a decent guy, just childish. We ended up falling out again and I got moved to a different cell.

I sold all my electronics for dirt cheap to focus on my main goal: get out of prison. I believed I had the smarts, but I had to shake the nonsense. This was the hard part. It worked for a minute. I got focused and went to work but still I was missing something. A vital part of the equation, so once again I fell off. I felt like I was stuck in a never-ending cycle. Something must give.

Eventually the whole state went on lockdown. During this time, I stayed high which you might expect, and it was free, so I wasn't losing anything. Yeah sounds good! I was truly at the bottom of the barrel. I was trying everything I knew how to do except the only thing that worked. Look at my truth and believe in myself. Sounds easier said than it was and right now I'm still shaking some of the misconceptions I've previously held.

But it got real one day, when I decided to take my life. I was finally accepting and proceeded to cut a vein in my arm in an attempt to end it all. It didn't work to my advantage like most of my ignorant endeavors. Story of my life. I felt like that epic failure was a sign to keep trying. I did and continue to have undesirable results. I had excellent ideas but no means to see them through. When I say hell, I truly mean I was in hell. From age 22 to 27 was horrible. Absolutely undesirable. It was a shame to see how far I'd fallen but I wouldn't give up.

I eventually found myself in the hole again. An everlasting cycle. I MUST BREAK THE PATTERN. This trip to segregation was different though it is a nine-month program called Intensive Supervision Unit. It is terrible. You level up every three months and gain your privileges back little by little. You have to get dressed by 8:00 AM, have your bed made and make your certain score in order to advance. The program is terribly unlawful. But I've seen the blessing in disguise. I can truly recreate myself with these nine months of isolation from the general population. It will still be a test and a different one indeed, but upon completion I plan to have all the knots sorted out. This is my chance. This is where it all turns around!

Chapter 4

Christopher

The Culmination

Phases is designed to break you and make you conform to the rules of the prison. It is made for you to do the most uncomfortable time possible. You are expected to be up and awake by 8:00 am with your bed made. You are not allowed to be under covers until after 5:00 pm. You are expected to be fully dressed in an uncomfortable yellow scrubs outfit at all times. No matter what the temperature is in the cell you are not permitted to be under covers until after 5:00 pm. You are only allowed 1 phone call per week after 6 months if you earned all your weeks. All of your personal property is taken and held until you are 6 months minimum into the program. Your family pictures are taken away. You are not permitted to order from the canteen. You are forced to survive only on state trays for 6 months. The program is one year-long. That is only if you go through it perfectly. Any infractions will set you back. Depending on what the infraction is, they will either hold your week back or start you all the way from the beginning. I've seen inmates stuck in phases for 3 years.

Every cell has a behavior sheet on the outside of the door. All the guards have to do is put marks on your board. Any marks on your board will result in getting held back in phases. You can get marks on your board for many trivial things, such as being asleep between the hours of 8:00 am through 5:00 pm, using sign language to communicate to other inmates across the pod or even not having your bed made a certain way. There is zero movement while in phases. The only time you get out of your cell is to take a shower, which is only offered 3 times a week.

When you are placed in phases you will have a celly (another inmate who lives in the cell with you). You have no control or say so in who you are placed in the cell with. The Facility profiles inmates and tries to match celly's according to race and gang affiliation. This process is highly ineffective because so many other things play into whether two inmates can live with each other or not. When I was first brought to phases I was put in the cell with someone I couldn't get along with. I asked the guards to move me out the cell. My request was not being taken seriously. This caused me to kick into survivor mode because every other day my celly and I were having arguments. I felt uncomfortable being in the cell with this person.

We are stuck around each other 24/7 and that is way too long to live in discomfort and uncertainty of your safety. The way the guards handle inmates in phases is before they open the door for any reason you must first be handcuffed from the food port on the door. Inmates often attack their celly's while the other one is in handcuffs.

You would think the guards will immediately open the cell door and break the fight up. This is not the case, instead they will just spray mace through the food port, inside the cell in an attempt to subdue the attacker. I've seen inmates able to fight through the sting of the mace and continue to attack their celly. So, in addition to being pummeled while your hands are cuffed behind your back, you're also being sprayed with mace.

I would not take the chance of being done that way. Feeling like I had no other options available to me, I skipped showers for a week and made a knife while my celly was taking a shower at those times. The next argument we had was because he didn't care about the condition of the cell and didn't care about getting marks on our boards for failure to have cells in compliance with the facility standards. I was not going to let him be the reason why I get held back in segregation longer than necessary. I tried to reason with him, but communication was difficult because it always leads to a hostile argument. I've had enough and decided this was the last argument. I told my cell mate one of us had to move immediately. When he told me that he was going to beat my ass, I pulled out my knife on him and told him I will kill him if he puts his hands on me. I told him "if you don't move out of this cell tonight, you won't make it to the morning." That finally got his attention. He had no idea that I had a weapon. We were able to gain the attention of the Sergeants on duty and let him know moves had to be done immediately or the situation was going to turn bad. We were both finally separated and put into two different cells. I was placed in the cell with a guy named Bobby Hilly. He was noticeably quiet and all he did was sleep and read. That was the perfect match up for me. It seemed like I could finally lay back, relax, and do time without some sort of drama.

For the first few months we hardly said anything to each other. I stayed to myself and he did the same thing. It gave me plenty of time to think and reflect on my life. As the weeks went by, I became increasingly depressed. Communication with my family is limited, I'm always hungry. I'm caged in a cell 24/7 and I felt as if my life will never amount to anything but prison. I felt like a failure and a disappointment to all of my loved ones. I felt alone. It seemed as if I was trapped in a concrete tomb and had no way out. The anxiety and the depression caused me to go days without sleeping. The insomnia was taking a toll on my mental state. I wanted to get out of my thoughts and be able to sleep. I requested to see the mental health Doctor. He prescribed me the proper medications I needed to numb my anxiety and to allow me to sleep.

Once I was able to sleep and think clearly, the harsh reality set in. The realization of how my life almost took me over the edge of insanity.

Brandon
The Culmination

As I stated in the last chapter, phases are a blessing in disguise, but this doesn't signify that it will be effortless. This is a true test that will push you to your limits. Phases is where the people that can't make it in the regular day-to-day prison lifestyle end up. The people who get write-ups excessively, get caught with knives or get class X's, the worst write up you can get. You won't understand what it is like until you live it, so borrow my eyes and see what I'm going through day-to-day.

First of all, what led me to this situation is a lack of self-control One day I felt good, working out and dancing around the pod. I do this ever so often; I love to dance and enjoy myself. But today was no different from any other day that I dance except for the small fact that a female correctional officer whom I don't particularly vibe with is working. We've had words on a few different occasions. But this day was the culmination.

This woman happened to open a cell door and stand in the direct path of the corridor where the inmates walk laps around the pod. I accidentally brushed against her and he said, "people have gone to segregation for less." Finally becoming fed up with her smart aleck comments I exploded. I told her I have 15 years and I don't give a damn about segregation. Then I walked off and continued to walk laps around the pod. She was still standing in the same place maliciously staring at me, which triggered the second outburst. This time, I repeated myself in a more aggressive manner. She then told me to lay down on the ground and I refused. By this time, the whole pod is watching. They have all laid down. Everybody is screaming and the pandemonium reached a pinnacle.

Refusing to get on the ground resulted in her spraying me with OC spray. This is an industrial pepper spray that is strong. After she sprayed me, I finally laid down. And for some reason in her head she continued to spray me. She called a response team and the response team handcuffed me and brought me to medical. There I decontaminated and waited for about 45 minutes to take a drug test. This time I had been sober for a while. So, while I'm sitting here waiting, I'm burning up, literally. Eventually I pissed and passed the test. They gave me clothes and took me to the infamous program. The Intensive Segregation Unit.

When I first arrived at this facility I was informed about the hell-hole of a "program." They told me it was all bad. No canteen, you have to be up by 8:00 AM. Just a bunch of frivolous rules. They told me you couldn't purchase hair products and people were so stressed they were going bald. Naturally, I didn't want no part of this program. So, I stayed out of trouble for as long as possible. While trying to rebuild myself. It was a fluctuating process that eventually led me to ISU.

When I got to ISU my suspicions confirmed everything, they told me it was true. They may have over exaggerated a slight bit but for the most part it was on point. Now imagine this: being locked in a 12x8x8 cell, no books, no extra food, nothing but your mat and blankets and clothes. The situation is so bleak and gloomy you immediately withdraw into yourself. You are being treated like an animal. Fed through a hole in the door called a bean hole. You have to be handcuffed to go to the showers, and the showers are a cage. To get a haircut you have to be placed in what is literally called "the cage." It is a degrading and humiliating experience that can either make you or break you.

Luckily for me though it was exactly what I needed. Though it is tough it gives me a chance to buckle down and look at life and my current situation. Knowing that I want something different in life I chose to fully embrace the situation and make the best of it. I chose to come out on top and take back my honor, self-respect, and dignity. I refuse to suck in wine all day but rather take this time to concentrate and remove the detrimental and unnecessary burdens from my life. Like I said this can either make or break me and I refuse to be broken. I will master myself and become victorious.

Now this is a difficult process. Nothing about being isolated and dehumanized is easy. It is in fact a long demanding journey. It's possible that anything can occur and if you allow yourself to fall victim you have to take steps backwards and redo something you have already done. The program in a hole is simple if you adhere to the rules. But the thing is they don't follow the policy guidelines themselves. they have a makeshift grading system that isn't in accordance with THEIR rules but expect the US to follow the guidelines. This in itself is a driving factor towards the madness. Now if I was ignorant to the situation it wouldn't matter but having an awareness of the situation makes it all the worse. Why? Because there is nothing worse than being aware of a wrong that's being done to you and not being able to fight it without seeing the light on the other side.

Believe me I have tried to fight and when it's one man fighting an army, it's kind of gets discouraging. But after a couple losses in re strategizing I have come up with a better plan to succeed. These people are all in cahoots and the people on my side don't want to change and the people on the other side don't want to allow them to change. It's like taking an army that doesn't want to fight onto a battlefield. The chances for victory are slim to none.

By the time I realized this I finally came to an understanding I must be a one-man army. I can't be the preacher and tell everybody that this should be how you live. No, I have to lead by example. My words are much more powerful if I have actions behind them. Success is a motivator. People are more inclined to listen to someone who is successful rather than somebody with just a good idea.

Therefore, I have to transcend these walls and the crazy ways they used to drive us insane. They literally play the same songs every week on a nonstop loop. People scream all day, lose their mind every day, fight and throw human waste on the staff. It's a madhouse. Another thing that drives people down the rabbit hole is not being in contact with their people. Some people don't have time to write letters and without the phone, that leaves you in limbo. You don't know what's going on, you don't have an idea how your family is doing or the latest developments. It gets real when you are all alone. You can stress and worry, and it can easily push you over the deep end.

A lot of people don't understand the negative environment that we are subjected to and because of our segregation from the general population they will never truly understand what we are going through in here. This is one of the greatest motivators for me co-writing this book. I want to help give people two perspectives to get a feel for what we go through in the prison system daily: our daily struggles and battles. How we can either be victorious or succumb to our circumstance.

One example of people losing their mind goes as follows. I was in the general population pod with this guy. He was your average gang member/prison inmate on my observation he was an alright kid. He played cards, walked around, and listened to music, minding his own business, and stayed to himself. Eventually, when I found myself in the ISU program, I learned he was also back here with me. As I settled in, I continued to hear someone screaming out of their door all day every day. I wondered who it was and ended up signing to another inmate across the way who told me it was the crazy guy in 105. With this statement I still didn't know who it was, but I definitely knew they were tripping.

One morning I happened to be up and not to my surprise, he was up screaming again. For what? I have no idea. Then the situation escalated. He took the bean hole (food port) hostage. This is when they open up your bean hole to serve you chow, and you stick your arm out and grab the hatch and refuse to allow them to close the door. He did this and they ended up calling the goon squad (a team in full body armor and riot gear that responds to situations that threaten security) By the time they came, the poor guy had already been sprayed with OC spray about 9 times. It was a bad deal, but he continued to buck. People are making bets on how long he will last. Some are encouraging him to keep going, some are telling him it's over with just cuff up. Meanwhile, his celly is still in the cell. He's already handcuffed and defenseless. So, while the instigator is continuing to take his stand. His celly is receiving all the backlash as well. The goon squad eventually extracted him from the cell and separated him and his celly. This is when I learned that it was this cool guy that used to be on the pod kickin' it. What had phases done to the poor guy?

A few more incidents like that follow. Taking the bean hole hostage. Then getting sprayed and extracted. He eventually moved closer to me. I could finally understand what he was yelling, and it just happened to be a bunch of nonsense. One time I caught something profound that he said that opened my eyes to something that I was trying to grasp. And in his insanity, he shined light on a truth that eluded me. He said "hey Ms. P. cell 212 is yelling for you, he probably needs something important, but cell 216 (his cell) is just yelling because he's in his head, and I don't like being in my head." You probably wonder what that means. What I gather from it is that in order to stay out of his mind and examine his life he would rather go crazy yell all day in order to avoid looking at the truth. Hearing that I immediately understood. People would rather live in this created world of theirs and entertain their delusions then come to the truth and change their wayward ways. It is truly sad if you think about it. People are so scared to be true to themselves because of fear of the unknown. Or what their peers may think. There may be multiple reasons they are reluctant to turn their life around, but it all starts with them and most are blind to this truth.

Like I said this program can either make you or break you. And I have witnessed people get broken with my very own eyes. I've witnessed people go from normal to crazy. I myself have watched my growth and am truly proud of myself for overcoming my negative circumstances. It is a daily struggle and one that I intend to win. One that I will win by all costs. And I hope my journey can show you that nothing is impossible, and you can overcome everything with a strong will and strong drive.

Chapter 5

Christopher

The Edge of Insanity

The medication that I was taking put me in a comatose, zombie-like state of mind. It made me feel numb to my surroundings. Although I was fully aware of what was going on, I became lost in my own mind. The dreams I had became very vivid. It was as if when I went to sleep, I was watching a movie in my mind. The movie of my life. I started to scrutinize every single aspect of my life examining every last detail. I felt like I was having an outer body experience watching my life through someone else's eyes. It brought me so much hurt and pain, I started to hate myself. The only people in the world who were in my corner and supported me with their blood, sweat and tears unconditionally I took for granted and even disrespected them when I was free. I spent a majority of my life fronting and faking who I really was. Blaming others for my bad choices and just in general was not the best person to be around. Too worried about portraying the "thug" image, I was losing sight of who I really was. I distinctly remember one dream that haunts me to this very day. It was like the "Christmas Carol". An evil spirit pulled me to the side and made me follow him around.

I remember asking him if I was dead. He looked at me and laughed and repeated his command for me to walk with him. He took me to an old run-down movie theater. We were the only people there and I wondered why he wanted me in this place. Out of nowhere the screen comes to life and I'm watching my life play out before my eyes. The evil spirit looked like he was enjoying the show. He had his feet propped up on the chair in front of him and was eating popcorn. I just looked on in complete shock as my life played in HD. I can see my parents working hard. Buying my siblings and I Christmas gifts, school clothes and taking care of us. I saw the family gatherings, the family vacations, and the wonderful times of my childhood. The movie was enjoyable to watch and it brought back many pleasant memories. Then out of nowhere, the movie started to take an unexpected turn. I saw myself at school acting like a "thug", fighting, and smoking and hanging out with other delinquents. I saw myself buying and selling drugs to people. I saw my parents crying and pleading with the judge on court dates. I saw the look on my mom's face when I got expelled from school. It made me sick to my stomach.

The spirit that was in the theater with me was laughing uncontrollably and eating his popcorn as if he were watching a comedy. I started to get scared. It just dawned on me that I may be dead, and this was my judgement. I stood up from my chair and made a run for it. As I ran out of the movies, all I heard behind me was a sinister laughter that frightened me. The door was locked. I was trapped inside the movies with this spirit and didn't know what would happen next. "The shows not over kid." was all the spirit said and continued to watch my life play out on the screen. I reluctantly sat back down and looked on as the screen displayed instant after instant where I've done despicable embarrassing things.

Then I saw something that made me want to call out to God for Mercy. I was in a casket at a funeral home watching my family weep over me. Everything happened in a fast-paced sequence. I was laid to rest underground and everyone left the graveyard. Life returned to normal and it seemed as if I never was even alive in the first place. I realized my life was meaningless and I've left no lasting impact on none of my family. Not my kids, my parents, or my siblings. My life was over, and it meant absolutely nothing. "Pointless ass movie if you ask me. I wouldn't pay to watch that again." The spirit broke me from my thoughts with this statement. I was speechless, hurt, and scared. I believed this was the moment where I'll go to hell. "You better get back to the drawing board kid, that ain't winning you any Oscars." Just like that he was gone. I woke up sweating profusely. For days, that dream played over and over in my head. I believed that there was way more to it than "just being a dream". I think that it was some sort of warning from God. I had mixed emotions of freight and relief of fear that I am on the path to hell and relief that I was given a warning and still had time to change the narrative of my life.

At this point, I have been in isolation for over a year and I feared I was losing my mind. I would dwell on thoughts excessively to the point where it consumed my entire day. I would spend weeks analyzing my life and trying to figure out all the things I've done wrong and all the signs I may have missed. I begin to obsess over knowledge of a higher power. In the past I didn't have much faith in religion. That changed when I had that dream. After that, religion became a subject I fixated on. I wanted confirmation on whether the medication was to blame for my dreams. Was I going insane or was a higher force truly trying to send me a message? I looked at my surroundings and I saw other inmates losing their minds. One in particular is a guy in a single cell who yells and talks to himself for hours on end. He refers to himself in the third person and the scariest part is I hear he never used to be that way prior to being in the hole. Being in long term segregation was eating away at his mind.

I was afraid I was going through a similar circumstance. I became angry and frustrated at feeling so confused and powerless. I challenged god. I told him "if you are real reveal yourself to me. I will believe in your existence only if you can show yourself in my dreams again." I wanted to have a deeper understanding of the world and my place in it. I needed answers.

The next few weeks I watched everything around me with a different eye. I became interested in every single thing that happened around me and wanted to know the cause for everything. If a guard was in a particularly good mood, I wondered why. If he was angrier than usual, then I wanted to know why. I felt that I was out of tune with the universe. That somehow, I failed to properly analyze my surroundings and adapt. I watched inmates get into it with each other and the police and I looked at the root of why these things would happen. The more I questioned everything around me, the more answers would come. It's as if I've been sleeping my whole life and now, I've somehow awakened.

The night that solidified, my belief in a higher power came to me in a dream. It was a direct answer to my challenge of god and his existence and power. The dream was a parallel of the one I previously had with the demonic evil spirit, except this one left me with a hope instead of fear. The most beautiful woman I ever laid my eyes on came to me and asked for me to follow her, that she had something special she wanted to show me. Curious and captivated by her beauty I obliged with no objection. We walked to what appeared to be a park. There were children running around everywhere. Cars parked all over. Concession stands selling cotton candy and popcorn. There was even a Jupiter Jump there where young kids were inside jumping and playing.

Curious as to where this place was, I asked the woman "where are we?" she replied in the most angelic voice I ever heard "we are all here to watch the show." Confused by this answer, I start to question her further when suddenly a huge screen appears. Everyone that was in their cars came out and started to sit on their hoods or in the bed of their pickup trucks. When I looked at the screen, I was flabbergasted to see that my life was what was being shown. Scene after scene it showed the moments of my life that I cherished. All of the special days from birthdays to regular movie nights with my siblings and parents. It brought back great memories and displayed the love and support that I always had. Then something very unexpected happened on the screen. As if the screen was a crystal ball instead of a movie screen, it started to show events which never occurred. I could tell it was the future because the ages of everybody in my family changed considerably.

My children were in their teens, my siblings were now mature adults, and my parents were older in retirement age. I saw myself on the tv with my daughter at her dance recitals. I saw another moment where I was with my son on a football field practicing passing routes with him. I saw myself visiting my parents and having wine and discussing life and making plans to expand our family business. I stared at the movie screen in awe transfixed at how meaningful my life seemed to be. It felt like my life had meaning and a purpose higher than myself. There was a man sitting on the hood of his car next to me and the angelic woman who brought me out to this outdoor movie. I overheard him telling his girlfriend that this was such a good movie he didn't want to get up and use the restroom.

The woman who I assumed to be an angel, nudged me with her elbow lightly. When I looked up at her all she did was wink. In the next instant I was awake and, in my cell, again. This dream left little to no doubt to me that there was a God, and that my life was being watched and judged. When I woke up that morning for the first time in a long time I felt at peace. There was a breakthrough being made and I decided that day, I will no longer take my medication. I just knew I no longer needed it. My mind needed to be clear. A deep desire burned within me to get a hold of my life and to start living with meaning and purpose. Even though the desire was there I still needed guidance on how to reconstruct my life from the ground up. I was set to do something I've never attempted doing before. Worry and doubt tried to show its ugly face and discourage me from embarking on my new journey. To align myself with the universe and walk as a righteous man. As if God saw my predicament he delivered.

A few weeks after having these dreams that awakened my spiritual self a book was delivered to me from my dad and mama T. The title of it is "Mind is the Master" by James Allen. This book is one of the most influential books I've ever read. Who knew that your whole life could change from one book? It is a self-help inspirational book that guides a person to live a righteous, happy, and fulfilling life. I began to read this book on a daily basis. It constantly kept my mind in the right place. I started to notice my mental health improve tremendously. My attitude improved; my thought patterns were changing. I knew I was over all on the right path to redemption and making the proper changes in myself to live a better quality, more productive successful life.

Brandon

The Edge of Insanity/Aware of my surroundings

Insomnia. It may sound like a minor problem but trust me that couldn't be any further from the truth. Naturally, I'm a night owl. I sleep during the day and work during the night. I have always been this way and probably always will, though I will change my schedule up if necessary. But eventually I will fall back into my vampire state.

I believe the reason for this is that I'm slightly introverted. I prefer to be alone with my thoughts and out of the loop of all the hustle and bustle most people are used to. When I'm up at night I don't have to deal with all of the nonsense that I'm usually subjected to being in the penitentiary. The yelling and screaming, the shower noises, the banging on the door. Nope, I sleep right through it and wake up at night to peace and quiet.

Now as I mentioned before, insomnia ain't no punk. Imagine being up for three days at a time unable to get a full night's rest.it is terrible and it does things to your mind. Your body goes into a hyper state, where it just wants to keep going and going. Sometimes I really feel like the energizer Bunny. I've wrestled with this insomnia for a while. No meds, no meditations, nothing will help. I will just remain awake praying for sleep. accompanying the insomnia is ugly old depression peeking his head in like "what's up old friend?"

113

Yeah, it's a mean combination; up for 12 hours with minimal rest, we'll just say 15-minute nap here and there then depression comes in with suicidal thoughts. I can remember days just tossing and turning for hours trying to grasp those sheep that kept eluding me. It really sucks.

The reason it sucks so bad is because with these mental illnesses comes a self-inspection. I would sit and think about all my past failures and search for the successes and I couldn't really find any. his was where I was really going to lose it. Sitting in this program trying to comply. Trying to fit my schedule with the program hours. Failing miserably. Something had to change. I don't know how long I could last. I try to use the medicine they gave me; it didn't work It made my mouth dry and made me dizzy. I even passed out completely once. Stood up, took a couple steps, and then woke up on the floor. I genuinely wanted to end my miserable existence. It just seemed like nothing worked and nothing was going to work.

I was disgusted with myself. I hadn't done anything worth being proud of my whole life. And I didn't know where to start. I knew I always wanted to help people and be there for my family, but I was just doing a poor job at it. I have tried to change my ways but failed at that too. So, I would just sit and wonder what next? And knowing myself. there is no telling what lies waiting around the corner.t

So yeah, I would sit and contemplate the world and universe and try to figure out what I was doing wrong, trying to find sleep and escape my depressive state.

I struggled with these thoughts for the first few months I was in this program. And It finally dawned on me, to be true to yourself. It happened during one of my insomniac depressive state I was going through. After being up for 2 1/2 days I finally broke down. I remember looking around for things to hurt myself with and couldn't seem to find anything sufficient for the task. I laid in my bed tossing and turning wondering why me? Why am I going through these hellish trials? What lies on the other side of all this suffering? I just couldn't figure it out. So, I humbled myself and asked the creator to help me. I remember saying "God, you know I have a good heart and you know my intentions are pure please help me, I can't do it on my own anymore." After that I dozed off after a 60-hour binge. When I went to sleep, I had one of the most vivid, touching dreams I've ever had. It was short but sweet. I was running through this fiery hell of a place struggling and thirsting for water. There were hellhounds and demons chasing and nipping at my heels. I was terrified. Pure horror wreaked around me from every angle. As I ran, I heard a voice from up above that trembled the ground like a ferocious earthquake "Just keep fighting you're almost done." I started to see something that shocked me to the core. The desolate wasteland ended, and I began to see a beautiful Oasis fit with the waterfalls and all. I gave it my all and continued to push. I thought my heart would explode; I ran so hard. But right when I neared the threshold I tripped. Story of my life. As I thought it was all over the voice chimed in again "leave him, he's mine." Right when the ghouls and goblins almost had me, the authoritative voice stopped them in their tracks, and they scurried back into the darkness. I got up still gasping for breath, running for my heaven. As I exited the hell, I jumped into a cool pool of the most crystal-clear water. I soaked in this healing spring while all my worries washed away with my pain. Again, the thunderous voice sounded off one last time. "Welcome to heaven on earth" it said. I woke up thrilled and even though I slept for about 15 minutes, it was some of the best sleep I have ever had. I felt rejuvenated and as I pondered on the most profound dream ever, the mail lady came with a book. This book changed my life, and I haven't looked back since. This book was called the "Millionaire Prisoner" by Josh Kruger and is one of the most powerful books I've ever read. Definitely in the top three.

In desperation I asked my momma to send me this book. I didn't put too much stock in receiving it because, I've been so detached from my family and haven't heard from my momma in a long time. But she came through and the universe aligned and delivered the book at the perfect time.

After this last bout of insomnia, I eventually went to sleep with a newfound respect for life. Upon my awakening I felt like a new man and I felt all my questions had been answered.

With this new perspective on life I adopted the mantra "Succeed or Die." I immediately began reading Millionaire Prisoner and scrutinizing the world with a predatory eye. I noticed everything was possible. I saw all the opportunities everywhere. Every interaction, every single second of every single day was a chance to take a step forward in life. I started seeing where I came from and all the possible come ups that I didn't recognize or squandered. I began to see all of my flaws. I slowly realized the place I was heading, and the place that I currently found myself in, I knew I had to make a U-turn and began re-routing. So, this is what I did.

As you've read, I was in a horrible place so maneuvering my way back out I knew was going to be an ordeal. I have to really dig in, stay down, and fully commit to the change. Considering the people, I was acquainting myself with I definitely had to modify my behavior. I was dealing with scumbags and you know what they say, birds of a feather flock together.

Noticing all the failures I committed. I wasn't going to allow myself to continue in the previous behavioral patterns that I followed. Just imagine all the money I could have made. All the places I could have seen. All the beautiful women I could have enjoyed. All this wasted time. But at last I learned my lesson; some people never get it. Now I look at my situation completely differently. I have examples all around me of who I don't want to be like. The majority of people in general pop are scared of change, so just imagine the one that's worried about being the oddball, the lone Wolf. I refuse to allow other people to control me. And I will be successful. There are no other options, point blank period.

Chapter 6

Christopher

Missing you Deeply

My Daily reading of Jamie Allen's "Mind is the Master" was exactly what I needed. It gave me a new outlook on life and helped me climb out of my depressive mind state.

One of the main things it says in the book that resonated with me is that "what you are, so is your world. Everything in the universe is resolved into your own inward experience. It matters little what is without, for it is all a reflection of your own state of consciousness. It matters everything what you are within, for everything without will be mirrored and colored accordingly." It goes on in further detail to explain that the perspective of how you view the world around you is the direct reflection of who you are within. The main point the book is trying to get across is that everything starts from within, and changes from within.

That message was extremely important to me because for the majority of my life I wondered why things would happen and why my world seemed bleak and overwhelmingly difficult. I honestly was able to come to the conclusion that it all boiled down to me and my perception. The character of who I was in my heart absolutely painted the picture of the world I saw around me. What it came down to was I had to start making some changes within my heart. That is, if I wanted my life to change.

This new line of thinking was a breath of fresh air giving me the positive results in my spirit and how I was dealing with doing time. I began trying to look at the lessons and the positive in every situation.

This new found wisdom had me feeling great at first, but as I felt myself grow in maturity and wisdom, I couldn't help but look back at my old self and feel tremendous pain, regret, and anger towards myself.

I was able to see how foolish and immature I was. I couldn't make excuses because I knew the truth.

As a man I did not cherish and honor my family as I should have. With all the unconditional love and support they provide me, I know I could have put forth more effort to be the best brother, son, father, grandson, nephew, and cousin I could be. I especially looked at my greatest supporters; my sister Krystle, my mama, Mama T, my dad, stepdad, and kids, know that thus far I have failed them. The absolute worst thing that you could ever do is take people for granted and I know that is what I've done. More than anything I wanted to change the course of who I was and make my family proud.

Since being incarcerated, I've seen the absolute worst things to happen to inmates in regard to their families.

There was one case in particular that I will never forget. The inmate's name was Landon, and he was around my age, maybe a year or two younger, his entire family; sister, little brother, mom, and dad were killed in an automobile accident. He was only 3 months away from being released and in an instant without warning his whole immediate family got taken away from him. I've seen other instances where were abused by boyfriends, daughters being misguided and mistreated by boyfriends, and son's getting murdered by gang violence. So many unfortunate circumstances that can happen to anybody at any time. All of these thoughts came into my mind and I grew fearful.

I realized life is not promised to us from day to day and that anything can happen at any time. My only prayer to God is to watch over my loved ones and to give me the chance to make my family proud and display the man that they deserve for me to be. My whole motivation for writing this book is to do something righteous that my family can be proud of.

I understand that I cannot change the past, however that does little to ease the pain that I still have for all the time I wasted and not putting forth my best efforts at being the son my mama raised. Embarrassing is an understatement on how I felt. Honestly, I was an emotional wreck. Multiple emotions ran through me as I grew more enlightened by the day. I know I was making progress though because I no longer was suicidal and depressed. If anything, I became more determined to make something positive out of my life, if it was the last time I do.

At 27 years of age, I couldn't believe how much time has passed. My family is growing older by the day. With each passing year my absence is having a greater impact on my loved ones.

I remember before I got arrested, my mother and I planned on repainting the inside of her home. I looked forward to the project with her, but my sudden incarceration delayed the endeavor. Almost 5 years later, the paint job still hasn't happened. That may sound trivial and petty, but I don't view it that way. My mom has tried to get her brother and different family members to help her paint her house, but there always seems to be some procrastination.

My loving, caring, righteous, sweet mother still has yet to get her house painted. After all the countless times I've witnessed her selflessly do for others, it angers me to an unreasonable height for reasons I still can't fully explain. It also saddens me because at the end of the day it comes back to myself. If I were there with her instead of wasting time away behind bars, that simple task would have been completed.

I look at my children growing up without a father present in their life, and it scares me. I feel helpless and frustrated that for the time being I have zero control or impact on the wellness and upbringing of my kids. There are many memories I know I've missed and there are times I can never get back. The gravity of that is not missed upon me. I fully understand the seriousness of me being incarcerated and how it affects not only myself, but my loved ones as well.

I get holiday cards with pictures of my family and to see that I'm not there, it aches my heart. It's hard to even look at my pictures. The majority of the time I have them put away and only pull them out to get momentary glances.

Every day I think about my family and wonder how their lives are doing. There's not a day that goes by that my thoughts aren't consumed by my loved ones and missing having a life again.

No matter how much I've changed my thought patterns and purified my heart, the changes cannot be validated or appreciated from where I am. I want to be able to heal all of the pain I've caused my family overnight. My rational mind understands that it will take time to cultivate my relationships how I desire them to do. However, with my understanding that life is not promised to anyone I feel it is imperative and urgent to do whatever it is that I can to demonstrate change.

Being incarcerated and watching your family suffer in any way being physical, financial, emotional, or spiritually is the closest thing to torture that I've ever experienced. It is a pain that never goes away. Every second of every I just sit and think everything over in my head and I grow frustrated. I feel like a helpless child who cannot feed himself.

The worst part of this pain is that I know fully that this is a self-inflicted wound. All of this grief and turmoil could have easily been avoided. The whole time I was out there selling drugs and living like I'm a trap rapper, I actually thought I was "cool", and that I was "the man". What a joke!

As I sat in my cell and continued to read "Mind is the Master", my spiritual self-started to awaken. I was truly asleep and had no real grasp on what it was to be an enlightened person.

Observations of my surroundings helped me solidify that I was done being blind. I would watch how inmates my parents age would be brainwashed from being in prison for too long. They were stuck on gang banging and foolery. It was sad. The lack of respect, intellect, social skills, and morals turned me completely.

I realized that if I continued to go down this senseless path of self-reflection, I would become just like one of these people.

A decision had to be made. I can either wallow in self-pity and not get anywhere or I can continue to strive to be the absolute best person I can be. I vowed to continually strive for excellence and not self-destruct. The place could either make you or break you. I refused to be broken. With the right attitude and mindset, success is inevitable.

An exercise that I read to do in "Mind Is the Master" was to plant as many positive seeds as possible whatever I want out of the universe. I must confess out of my mouth. When you ask God and the universe to provide your desires they will do as long as you remain righteous.

My mentality was "to get what I've never done", so with this new approach I ceased all frivolous conversations and thoughts. The only words that I speak will be pure and righteous. This was a daily practice that I tried with hopes of positive results.

My desires are to be the best man I can be morally, spiritually, and financially. I want to provide for my family and make an honest genuine change from my heart. To become pure hearted, I would know I am fulfilling my purpose in life. My little sister Krystle is the best example I can give of being pure hearted. She is a great inspiration to me, and I've seen how she makes my parents proud. I want to mirror her characteristics and evolve.

The person I used to be is not appealing to me. The beauty of life and being a creature of consciousness and intelligence, is we have the ability to evolve and change at will on everyday basis. We do not have to be stuck to one particular mind set of attitudes. We can recreate ourselves at any time of our choosing. God gave us the ability to be whomever we decide to be.

With only one year left on my sentence, I know I must prepare myself the best way possible for success upon release from prison. Failure and recidivism are not an option!

With nothing but time on my hands, I have decided to use it to the best of my ability. One way I wanted to prepare myself was to write down a specific, realistic, and detailed plan on how I planned on reintegrating back into society. With the belief that I cannot do anything in my current circumstances, all of my plans were starting from when I got released. The only thing in prison I felt I could do was get my mind right and have a solid game plan for when I get released.

God showed me I was wrong. He heard my desires and saw my motives and knew my intentions were pure. He provided me with insight that changed my life instantaneously and expanded my mind to a world of new possibilities that never occurred to me before. The light I stumbled across came from the most unexpected and darkest place.

Brandon
Missing You Deeply

Going through these changes and maturing you start thinking about what truly matters in life. The times wasted, the people you took for granted, the immature lifestyle you led. All these things become evident because you begin looking at life with truth.

I truly feel like a piece of shit because I forgot all about my family and only called or talked to them when I needed them. I was selfish. All the love that I said I had for everybody was just that, something I said, my actions didn't portray my words but rather betrayed them. I could have had as many good memories as possible with my family and friends if I wasn't living in La La land completely oblivious to what truly mattered in life.

But that's the beauty of enlightenment: you become aware of truth. A very powerful, if not the most powerful, element in the universe. You are able to see through clear eyes and begin to move in accordance with your destination. This process of enlightenment self-realization eventually jolted me out of my delusional state and allowed me to become a real man. As a real man reality hit me like a kamikaze bomber. After 27 years I have done nothing to make my family proud. I have a son and nieces and nephews. I must handle my responsibilities. I have to be the difference. I have to set the example. I have to be the leader to my family.

With this awakening I began to long for my family, missing them deeply. I started reminiscing about my childhood and spending time with my mom and dad grandma and grandpa, uncles, cousins, aunts. It was evident that somewhere I made a wrong turn and veered off course. I eventually put all my pictures away because just looking at them made me think of how I failed the ones I loved. Those pictures were definitely a contributing factor to the depressive states I often found myself in. I just didn't know how I was going to come back from all this turmoil and let down. But ask and you shall receive! The universe eventually aligned and gave me a road map that led me out of the land of sorrow to heaven on earth.

One of my biggest regrets though is missing my little boy. I hate the fact that I was immature and had a son while I was still a child myself. Because of my wrong decisions, I haven't been able to be there for him like a father truly should. Every day I think of my little sunshine and it eats me up that I was too selfish to put him in the first. I remember when he was just a baby and we would kick it and I would play with him all day. I remember his beautiful smile and him calling me daddy.

I remember when he first started talking and his love for dogs. It made me so proud to have a little me and be able to watch him grow up. I was young and honestly, I was scared. I didn't know what I was doing and whatever I was trying to do wasn't sufficient. So, I sit here and just think. My son is the main driving factor for the changes I'm making in life. Every child deserves a father and I vow to be one whether incarcerated or free. I have no room left for mistakes. It's terrible that it took all this time to make me realize what's important in life. But again, at least I did. Some people never do. Just writing this tug at my heartstrings. It definitely puts me in my feelings, but I do it all for you son. Every day I think of you and you inspire me to be the best man I can be. I pray you don't lose faith in me son. I'm working hard to return to you as soon as possible. I love you little boy.

Now about my parents. I watched these people make so many sacrifices for me in order to provide a decent living environment. I thank them for all their efforts. I know it may seem that I'm ungrateful, but I am very grateful. I just didn't know how to show it. I was lost and confused, and it never dawned on me that I was so far from the truth. I appreciate everything you all have done for me and though I won't wasn't shit, excuse my language, I have grown to be a real man and I wouldn't have made it this far if it wasn't for y'all. Thank you for all the hard work, good times, bad times, parent teacher conferences, football practices and games. Just thank you so much. Sitting back thinking, all I can do is admire my parents. Though we weren't rich we were comfortable. And that was due to their devotion.

I have some beautiful childhood memories with my family. One of my earliest ones is when my dad dressed up as a clown for my birthday. I remember it so vividly; it was me and my older cousin's birthday party. I was probably 3 and she was maybe four. I can't remember for sure. Yeah but there were balloons everywhere, all my cousins were there and then this big goofy clown came out. My dad. We loved it. We laughed until we couldn't anymore. Then we ate cake and opened presents. It was a wonderful time and I miss having all my family together like that.

I remember having movie nights, eating caramel popcorn. I remember going to the drive-in movies, getting doused in mosquito repellent, stocking up on snacks and tuning into the radio station that provided the audio for the movie. My childhood was good. My people tried hard to raise me the right way and I had many amenities that some people only dream of. Somewhere along the line I decided to rebel though. In my stubborn little mind, I believed I was doing something cool, but I was really disgracing my family. One of the ten commandment states "honor your mother and father so that you may live a long time in the land that Jehovah, your God is giving you."

I guess it's all about perception though. I was childish. I couldn't quite grasp the concept of being a man. Plus, I was terrified of responsibility. Growing up I didn't picture myself with the car or house or paying bills. I didn't know where I was headed but I kept this delusion in my head that somehow, I was going to be a famous rapper.

Now that I've gone through, I accept the responsibilities and in order to honor my parents I have to step up to the plate and knock it out of the park. There is only room for excellence. No more time for satisfactory performance. I owe it to my predecessors.

I watched my parents' struggle. Just to make sure I was fed so I will pass my knowledge and wisdom to the next generation in an attempt to guide them around the failures I've experienced an observed other people succumb to.

My grandparents are another example of people I took for granted. They have always been around for me and in my life ever since I was young. I didn't realize how valuable an asset they were until my recent awakening. It finally dawned on me that they are excellent sources of wisdom and I never thought to tap that well. I would have avoided a bunch of heartache if only I sought out their wisdom.

Even though this revelation hit me so late down the line it still is a profound discovery. Now I am a true seeker of wisdom and truth. And I will find what I'm looking for by remaining diligent and vigilant. There is no such thing as too much knowledge and it is said that gray hairs are a crown of wisdom. Now I hold the utmost respect for my elders including the ones I have no blood relation to.

The value of generational wisdom is priceless. And I can't thank my grandparents enough for the exemplary example they have set. I also enjoyed some beautiful times with my grandparents. For example, I used to spend the night over my grandma's and watch horror movies all night. She would always fall asleep on me and I would end up finishing them myself. By the time she would wake up, I would be ready to sleep myself and I would go cuddle up in bed with her. When we woke up, we would cook breakfast together. She recently wrote to me and told me she thought I would grow up to be a Chef. It was a career I pursued but it was snatched from under me, but that's another story entirely.

My grandma used to be a lighthouse to me, and now that I've shaken the stupor, she still is. She's an awesome, loving woman. She's Godly and driven. Thank you for all the lessons you've taught me, directly and indirectly, they are truly invaluable.

The same respect goes to my grandpa. He is a retired firefighter. He's risked his life saving people, being valiant and strong. He is a great inspiration in my life and now I can see the burning fire in my heart that I must stoke and care for in order to lead an adequate lifestyle. Yeah, my granddad is an amazing man and as he rises in age, he still is a great example of how a man should compose himself.

The things he taught and trained me protected me these prison walls and are a sword that accompany me along my journey to conquer manhood. It may appear that I have been ungrateful and maybe I was, but now I truly hold my ancestors in great reverence considering all the time and effort they committed in order to keep our family intact. It's truly a blessing not only to have these people in my life, but to also realize the struggle they have been through and the triumph they have received along the way. These are true family jewels.

While on the subject of family I must not forget my siblings. I shared tons of memories with my little brother and sister. We grew up fighting and arguing, loving, and hating and I have unlimited love for them. I admit I wasn't a good example to follow growing up and in my early adulthood. I am extremely apologetic for not being the big brother I should have been and it hurts me deeply to know that I failed my duties as an older brother, but I vowed to make it up for the remainder of my life.

Running around the house playing hide and seek, outside playing with bugs and getting dirty in the mud. These are all fine memories, and I wouldn't ask for anybody else to share them with but them. That time we got covered in mud after it had been raining for days. Mom's reaction was priceless. Man, good times, but me being the ringleader I always got the brunt of the discipline. I really miss my siblings. I will make sure the example I set from now on is outstanding. I truly apologize for my inadequacy and strive to do better. To my brothers and sisters, I didn't grow up with, I haven't forgot about you all and miss you as well. I pray this book will help bring us all closer. We are all we have.

Last but not least are all my aunts, uncles, cousins, friends and everyone else who helped me or on my journey. I deeply miss you all and all of the good times we've shared. I am grateful for the imprints you've left on me and thank each and every one of you. It is a blessing that you have been here with me and watched me evolve.

Part II

Cognizance At Last

Chapter 7

Christopher

Finding Light in the Darkest Place

While studying and meditating in my cell, I heard inmates talking in the vent. I usually tune out the people who talk on the vent because in most cases they are not talking about anything of importance and value. I already told myself I would not engage in any frivolous conversations and activity, so I became antisocial. Being that I am in such a negative environment, me making the change I decided to make automatically classified me as a minority, so I prepared myself to travel on my journey alone.

The conversation I heard taking place caught my attention for two reasons. One, the person who was talking was speaking about positivity which is a rarity, and he mentioned a book he has that changed his life. The title is "Millionaire Prisoner". This instantly piqued my curiosity. The second reason I tuned into the vent was because of who I discovered was talking. That person was Brandon (Bad Wolf) Nelson. He was on the same pod as me when we were on the main compound in general population. My first impression of him was that he was crazy. I thought he was insane by the way he carried himself and the things he would do. He is certainly one of the strangest people I've ever met. He carried himself like a modern-day hippie, reminding me a lot of a mix between Jimmie Hendrix, Andre 3000, Prince, and Young Thug. Bad Wolf would be in a drug induced state and rap/dance for hours non-stop. The whole pod would always get a good laugh from watching him on the yard bare footed chasing butterflies or doing kung-fu randomly.

Bad Wolf always seemed to be lost in his own world and I just wrote him off as being a man who has lost his marbles. The last time I saw Bad Wolf was the day he was sent to long term segregation. I'm not clear on the exact circumstances which lead to him being put in phases. I just remember seeing him getting sprayed with mace point blank range. He seemed to not be affected by the mace in the least bit. He laughed and howled at the COs as if he were an actual wolf.

The person I was hearing on the vent was a totally different person from the one I remembered on the pod. Even though we never spoke to each other much, we were cordial and knew each other.

I overheard him telling a dude named Simba on the vent that he was done with illegal endeavors because logically it just didn't make sense. He was speaking in a highly intelligent way that shocked me. He was very bright, and I knew that I had the wrong impression of him. Simba kept trying to argue the point that some crimes are necessary to do if you're put in a certain situation. I intentionally listened as Bad Wolf made logical points supporting the idea that under no circumstances is engaging in illegal activities an acceptable answer or even worth it.

I agreed with him and wanted to give my thoughts on the subject. I am not sure why I felt compelled to even contribute to the conversation, but I went with my inner intuition and joined in. I stated that "hustling to support " your family was a bogus excuse to illegally sell drugs. At the end of the day, when you get caught and have to sit down for years of your life, how would you "support your family" then?" This idea was immediately rebuked by other inmates on the vent and after a while I grew tired of going back and forth over the subject. I already had my mind made up of the matter and wasn't swaying away from it. If others disagreed, then that was okay with me. I'll just continue to do my own thing.

Before I decided to leave the vent, I told Bad Wolf "it's good to see I am not alone in here. I was beginning to have my doubts". He replied back "Now bro, I'm definitely on the path to righteousness, that's the only way to survive". "I couldn't agree more" I conceded with him. I was still curious about the book he said he was reading "Millionaire Prisoner". The title grasped my attention and I had to know what it was about. Being that his mindset was similar to my own, I saw an opportunity to trade off books. I told him that I had an excellent read that will help make him a better person, and that I will trade it for his book, and we can switch back out in one week. He agreed to this and we made the trade through the C.O.

The second I received the book I went to work reading it, not wanting to waste any time being that I only had one week to read it. Amazing will be an understatement of the impact that "Millionaire Prisoner" had on me. The enlightenment and wisdom the book gave me literally changed my life and boosted me to an even higher level of understanding than I was already on from reading "Mind is the Master".

"Millionaire Prisoner" is a nonfiction book about a prisoner serving a life sentence who has become a self-made millionaire legally from within his cell.

He gives numerous and specific examples of how you can turn your cell into an office or classroom. With no technology at your disposal and having to rely on an outside network and mail correspondence only, he gives you invaluable knowledge on how to wisely invest your time and money. Not only does he just give you advice, but he also goes a step further and gives you specific resources that help you to achieve your goals.

Reading "Millionaire Prisoner" was yet another answer to my prayers. God revealed himself to me again. It's as if God and the universe were leaving me little breadcrumbs that will lead to something much greater.

One of my biggest burdens was feeling helpless and powerless from my confinement. I was tired of feeling useless, not being able to do anything of importance or value myself or family.

After four years of being taken care of by my family and not being in my kids' lives, I wanted more than ever to be productive in any possible way than I can.

I finished reading the book after only three days. My mind was spinning with the new world of opportunities I now can see. My family is incredibly supportive, and I know if I presented any legal ideas to them, they would support me without hesitation. It blew my mind that I've never had the opportunities that were before me the whole time. Now that I am aware of how I can utilize my time to its maximum potential there was no turning back.

"Mind is the Master" helped me awaken my spiritual self. "Millionaire Prisoner" helped me transcend my mind outside of the box I lived in. My new attitude was to do something now!

I decided to read the book again just to fully absorb all the knowledge it had to offer.

After going over the book twice, I made a list of all the possible things I can do from within my cell realistically that would be productive and produce an income.

With my access to the phone being non-existent due to me being on Phase 1 in the phase program, the only communication I had with my family was through letters. This made it even harder to try to start a business venture, but I was motivated and determined to make something happen. I will not accept excuses or failure.

After the weekend, Bad Wolf and I switched our books back. We began discussing what we had learned from the books we traded and how we felt about what we read.

I told Bad Wolf that those two books alone changed my life. I said "Mind is the Master" was for the mind, and "Millionaire Prisoner" was for the grind. Knowing what I know now how can I go backwards?" He responded that he felt the same way.

As the conversation progressed, we started bouncing ideas off of one another. We both decided that we didn't have anything to lose, but everything to gain. We wanted to put forth the action and not just "talk the talk". All we were lacking was the right idea of what could be done given our situation.

Bad Wolf asked me if I realized how crazy it was how everything fell into place. How being in long term segregation strengthened us and made us overall better than we were before. He asked if I believed in coincidences. I told him I did not believe in coincidences, because from a logical view point it just doesn't seem possible.

There are thousands of things that occurred in a unique sequence in order for us to be in the exact predicament we are in. If one single thing changed then the entire outcome would have been different. A coincidence to me is like throwing 1,000 different unassembled pieces of a clock in the air and they land in perfect sync producing a fully functional clock.

When I said this to him, something clicked in my head like the light bulb went off. We both have inspiring stories that talk about our separate journeys that lead to redemption and salvation. Thus, the idea of "Conversations Through The Vent" was born.

Brandon

Finding Light in The Darkest Place

S itting in this program stressing and missing my family led me to reach out. I reached out to my grandma on a whim really asking for moral support and trying to strengthen our relationship. I also asked for some help financially if possible and asked for two books. One of those books helped change my life forever. That was the millionaire prisoner.

After I received it, I read it incessantly, soaking in the knowledge and wisdom it contained. It validated a lot of the previous notions I held and proved to me that I wasn't really crazy just vastly misunderstood. It basically touched on every aspect of life I was trying to correct. From appearance to making money, morality to building a network. It proved to be an excellent tool to me. Not only did it support the new lifestyle I was trying to create for myself but helped eradicate any delusions that I continued to hold. The book was so profound that after I read it once I meditated on it and began immediately implementing the lessons into my life.

After I digested it once, I returned for seconds and planned on scrutinizing every detail in the book. I began reading and highlighting the applicable points in the book just as it instructed. While studying I happened to take a break and commune with my neighbor about the lightbulb that went off in my head. I relayed to

143

him the fact that I was done with the illegal lifestyle and decided to live my life righteously. Considering the place, we are in I definitely expected my new stance in life to be met with opposition, and that it was. We had a civilized debate about the circumstances where it would be justifiable to resort back to illegal methods in order to procure means. Some of his points were family matters if somebody said so and so about me or did such and such to me. I remained steadfast in my stance. With the resolution I received I knew that in order to be untouchable I had to operate in the boundaries of the law. We continued to argue until Christopher joined the conversation. He immediately took my side and validated that by no means is it acceptable to take penitentiary chances.

I was surprised by his input, because I didn't believe there were more people that believe like me especially in the penitentiary. After our initial conversation we began to become well acquainted. He mentioned he thought I was crazy which didn't surprise me by how I previously conducted myself.

We hit it off and began conversing about positivity. I mentioned that I had this book I was studying that was so good that I had to immediately reread it. He was adamant about reading it as well because the title supposedly intrigued him. I was reluctant to share this book because it was truly one of the most inspirational books I've ever read. He continued to ask for it and said he had a book that he would trade with me. I was skeptical because I hold myself to a high intellectual standard and most people don't reach it. But finally, I relented, and we traded. Boy, was I glad we did.

The second most profound book I've read. And the most enlightening. This book literally rocked my foundation and was the final piece of the puzzle I've been putting together my whole life. This book is called Mind is the Master. I can't over exaggerate how important this book is to me. It literally destroyed all the questions I had about religion and spirituality. It supplied me with the truth I've been seeking and gives no room for speculation. I adopted it as my new Bible. I chose not to read it straight through but instead just open up the book and start reading. I couldn't go wrong with this approach considering the fact that every page contained divine knowledge.

This may be controversial to some considering their strict adherence to a certain religion, but it definitely enlightened me to true spirituality after many years of searching. With these newfound books it finally sunk in and so did I. I stood firm in my resolve and decided finally I was done with the old me. I continued to study and correct, study and correct and the more this occurred the better I felt. I wiped the clouds out of my eyes and pushed forward. The Mind is the Master helped reveal the path I was determined to find and showed me that my mind state was in the right place and my actions were sure to follow. It turned out that my internal and external studies of the universe seemed to pay off.

The more I conversed with Christopher the more I became sure. We continue to build and strengthen each other, and he provided an extremely bright light for me to level with and I couldn't thank him enough. Witnessing his struggle helped me realize where I was falling short. And having someone to talk to about these types of things was monumental. Christopher eventually came up with an idea to write a book based on the profound experience we shared. We talked about it and juggled ideas back and forth and finally came up with the conclusion. Thus, Conversations Through the Vent was born.

CHAPTER 8

Christopher

Blood Is Thicker Than Water

It has been a long and arduous journey through my incarceration. I have literally been through hell and back. I've lost myself completely and come back from oblivion.

My faith in God had been restored and my mind is sharper now than it has ever been before. There are a few people in my life I must give credit and praise for being the driving force that allowed me to beat the statistics and make it through my trial and tribulations in one piece.

Through it all, these people have supported me every step of the way. Never did any one of them turn their way back on me or give up on me. That would be my family. My little sister Krystle, my mama, mama T, and Dad. There have been others that helped along the way, but these four people are the reason why I have not perished. They believed in me. When I didn't have the strength to believe in myself. Their unwavering love gave me the strength I needed to keep pushing forward.

My family's love detoured me from joining any kind of prison gang. I refused to give my loyalty to or align myself with

147

such a group of unloving and counter product people. If anybody deserves my loyalty and one hundred percent commitment., it would be my family.

A memory I will never forget is when my mom got laid off from her job. I didn't know it at the time, because she doesn't want me stressing over family matters, I have no control of. I needed money on my books to purchase hygiene and food, so I asked my mom if she could put money on my books. She said to me "Alright Christopher I'm going to put $50.00 on your books, but you need to make it last for a while until I can figure some things out. I don't have my job anymore and only have $100.00 to my name right now. Krystle is helping my with things until I can find another job" This revelation hurt my soul to the core, that my mother was in such a condition and that instead of me being able to aid and provide relief to her, my little sister is left to put together the broken pieces and carry my slack. To make things worse Krystle is still holding me down financially. She did so with no complaint or no excuses- not even one time.

I was grateful, proud and appreciative for Krystle and all her sacrifices, but it also was a constant reminder of how I put myself in this unnecessary predicament and also what I should be out in the world doing. I also remember when I was in Kansas being held in the hole for over a year. I was losing my mind to the point of talking to myself. My mama T and Dad did everything they could do to keep me from losing my mind. They kept money on the phone so I could call them daily and have someone to talk to. My Dad gave me a schedule to live by to keep my day active, productive, and busy. They would send books and letters often. They honestly went above and beyond for me going the extra mile to ensure that my mental health stayed intact.

My mother and sister Krystle traveled from Alaska and Oklahoma City to Northern Kansas in Norton where I was being held, just to see me with their own eyes and check on me. They told me they didn't like how I sounded on the phone, it worried them to the point of them deciding they had to come up and see me for themselves and verify that I was ok.

Memories like those will never escape me. My family genuinely cared about me when I didn't even care about myself. Realizing the love and support I had from my family, I instantly stopped caring about trying to be a "thug" or trying to uphold some sort of image of me being a "gangster." The only people I aspire to impress or gain approval from, is my family. To have went through everything I endured and still continue to fake like I still want to affiliate with the streets will be idiotic and foolish. I've come way too far to go backwards, and I owe it all to God and my family.

Showing my family that everything they have invested in me did not go to waste is very necessary and important to me. Implementing my changes and living a righteous, prosperous life would be a great victory. Realizing the power of love and support, knowing how it saved my life numerous occasions, has set a standard for me. This is the same type of love and support that I need to be giving my kids. My children deserve an active father in their lives to guide and lead in the right path. They should not have to travel down the same treacherous path of misery that I did.

The "Christmas Carol" type dream that I had will always be a motivator for me to step my game up in every way. I've seen what the overcome would be if I failed to handle my responsibilities. I believe God showed me this for a reason. I've seen a countless number of people who do not have families, or a positive support system. This is one of the main causes for them to seek refuge from gangs.

What people should know and understand fully, is that there is no love, no support, no salvation, or no prosperity to be obtained by joining any gang. Even with no family, there are many other resources that someone can use to network with positive, uplifting people. Churches, social groups, business associates, professionals, car clubs, and the book clubs are just a few places one could look to network with the right people.

Sharing my story with others, I hope to inspire, encourage, and motivate people who have found themselves in situations similar to my own. I want to become a source of positive support and guidance, the same way family has done for me, seeing how much of an impact it had on my life showed me how important it is to reach out and care for the next person.

It's crazy to think how something as simple as letting someone read an inspirational book can have the power to change lives.

Blood, as referred to in the chapter title represents love, support, inspiration, guidance, and motivation. Water represents the negativity, false support, malicious intentions, and counterproductive activity. Water flows recklessly and takes many different forms; however, blood is the lifeline, and flows directly to the heart, and is indeed thicker than water!

Brandon

Blood Is Thicker Than Water

While writing this book I began to come up with a resolution. I've been through some things in life and I've accumulated a perspective that allows me to be real with myself and the judgments I make. Examining the nature of my peers and how they operate has allowed me to discover what's important in life. I was guilty of living this false life that didn't honor the only people who truly cared for me. My family.

I used to try and be a gang member, a blood to be specific. Living this lifestyle, I never fit in, I always stood out, being different and adhering to a certain moral code. I tried to justify my actions and continue to keep my loyalty to this faction knowing it was holding me back from my true potential. I was representing an entity that didn't hold the same values as me, so I was basically trying to serve 2 Masters at once. Which is impossible. Struggling with this inner demon for years I continued to find myself in situations that I knew I should not have been in.

I never found violence appealing or praying on the weak. His was not how my mind operated and it went against my nature. I do believe in self-defense, but not frivolous violence. And the fact that I have to allow a single word to control me was completely illogical. For years I've wrestled with myself over this matter. Time after time beating myself senseless trying to subdue the ignorant self and allow the true self to thrive.

Eventually I came to. After being taken to "court" and shunned, after continuous disagreements with the homies, after multiple physical altercations with the people who were supposed to be on my team, I finally had enough. I eventually broke up the ties with the gang and tried to restore my relationships with my family.

It dawned on me who the ones where I truly should be fighting for. The people who have worked hard just to get me to this point, the people who have fought through blood, sweat and tears, the ones who have made sacrifices for me to be able to live, the people who truly love me. This is where my loyalty should have been the entire time but being young and dumb, I didn't ever truly grasp the profundity of family I took them for granted. Luckily, I haven't suffered any losses and still have a chance to refurbish all my relationships. This is truly a blessing because some people don't have this revelation or if they do, they don't have the opportunity to do it because it is too late.

Therefore, my family deserves all my time and effort knowing that I have a limited time here with them and knowing they are the ones that have my back. When I was young my mother and father were highly active in my life, making sure I would be prepared to succeed. When I was just four, they had me tested and enrolled in a French immersion program where I study French for 10 years of my life. In my early years I excelled in school at the top of my class, but slowly began to decline.

I eventually became indifferent to education and fell off. Academics seemed to become redundant. I felt like I was in an everlasting loop of monitory. I quit doing homework, quit studying, and just goofed off in class. I started getting into trouble and began leading the life of a troubled youth.

I received plenty of discipline and this was just fuel to the fire. It caused me to be more rebellious. That and watching my parents fight and argue with each other added to my distress and I just wanted to escape reality and cease to exist. During my junior high and high school years my dad was my football coach, so he was a constant presence. Pushing me harder and harder to succeed. But the more he pushed the farther I fled. I began gang banging in junior high portraying this image that I was some tough guy when I really was a little church boy. My parents continued to try and straighten me out, but it never worked.

I remember running away from home and living in the streets. I was just spitting in my parent's face. After all the effort they put toward me, I failed them. As I hung around in the streets, I constantly found reminders that the streets didn't love me. The people I called friends, the women that I had relationships with, they didn't love me they just wanted what I had to offer at that time. As soon as I didn't have what they were looking for they kicked me to

the curb. Now I have a few friends that stay down, and I consider them friends. But the rest of them flaked away like de skin never to be seen or heard from again.

It's basic math 2 + 2 = 4 and if you lead a fake life you w attract fake people. It shouldn't have taken me this long to realiz this truth, but it did, and I believe in divine timing. All lessons are to be learned in their respected season, and finally grasping this concept I knew I had to make changes to my life if I wanted to save the relationships that really mattered. So I searched inward for my true heart and prayed that God would strengthen me and straighten my path out in order to honor the ones that raised me and the younger generations that will come after me. For these people I am willing to fight for and give my life. It's not just the blood that I share with my family it's the blood I share with humanity and Mother Nature. I know I am better than hiding in the background and acting like I don't know the truth.

As I look back in history, I have great examples of powerful men who have fought for their people righteously. 1 great role model is Malcolm X. Being a part of an organization Malcolm rose to the top ranks and began leading his people with efficiency. He rallied the troops and fought for what he believed in. He was a righteous man and through adversity sealed his name in the history books. Once he figured out the truth, he didn't run from it or try to hide it, he embraced it and exposed it. He provided a perfect

illustration of what a leader should be like, and how a man should compose himself.

With giants like Malcolm X to follow I can't allow myself to excuse the truth and go about like it doesn't exist. I must be a bright beacon for the people and youth who are continuously misled from the truth. As I mentioned, this doesn't include just the people I share genes with, this is much larger than immediate family, and even humanity, and this is for the blood I share with life. Every living creature deserves the best we can provide. Every single second provides an opportunity to do something good. Every single second we can either move forward or backwards. Every single second we should be striving for justice.

To waste opportunity is to truly blaspheme. If you look at the situation from a perspective of truth you will understand the fact that if God gave you an able body and sound mind and you choose to be idle you are squandering the blessing that God has given you. Understanding this I prefer to make the most out of my life and continue to reap and sow the seeds in the product of righteousness.

I have this theory, that if you live within the boundaries of righteousness you can't be touched, mentally, physically, or spiritually. What brought me to form this theory is this: living righteously involves remaining on the right side of the law which helps you remain untouchable mentally because it takes away from this stress and worry that you may be caught by the authorities and

subjected to the revocation of your freedom; I believe it allows you to remain untouchable physically because as a righteous man or woman you are going to make sure your temple is clean and held in the highest standard possible, eliminating the chance of disease an physical misfortune Spiritually untouchability comes in this form, holding and keeping a certain moral code which you value and adhere to. Doing this you're not blown from idea to idea, you won't entertain foolishness and you will avoid all wickedness. Through my predecessors and the other great examples in history I have been able to witness people who are immovable and untouchable and following their lead I continue to strive for this untouchability.

There are millions of people that would do better if they knew better and a lot of them are misled by the people that they choose as role models. There aren't enough people out there practicing and preaching righteousness a lot are selling false dreams that consequently lead you to prison and end up getting you killed. These are all reasons I chose to change my life and become a leader instead of a wayward follower. The boys and girls who believe that they can make it big by living a street life, my family who have struggled to support me when nobody else would and God who has blessed me with a beautiful mind and viable body I used to try and be a blood, but now I honestly represent blood. No not the gang that operates off of negativity but the blood that was shared by the people who came before me in order to allow me to live a comfortable life. The blood that I share with my mother, brother, sister, aunts, uncles, grandparents, and cousins. The blood that flows through my veins that I was graciously blessed with and the blood of the future generations that will succeed me. Once again, the cliché rings true: blood is thicker than water!

CHAPTER 9

Christopher

The Vent Talks

This newfound benevolence formed between Bad Wolf and I lead to many ambiguous discussions on the vent. We would stay up for days at a time analyzing our lives, society, the prison system, the world, the universe, God, family, and various other topics. No subject was off limits. With a revitalized perception and mindset. I saw everything with a different eye.

The objective behind wanting to examine certain topics was to gain a deeper understanding and ultimately eradicate any chance of recidivism. Studies show that approximately 85% of offenders come back to prison. Most people I've talked to, have been to prison numerous times. On a few occasions I have seen people myself discharged then come back shortly after being released.

I simply cannot allow for this to become my reality, so I must drastically find the solutions and do what others aren't doing, by identifying the most common downfalls. My desire for seeking truth allows me to analyze myself and others in an unjustifiable manner. Excuses and passing blame will not keep me out of prison! I want results.

159

It's as if I were born again and was discovering things for the first time, like a curious child. We both were now fully spiritually awakened, so we found joy in going over every possible topic to discover new knowledge we weren't able to see before or completely missed when we're living in a spiritually slumbered state. There's a great difference between knowing something, and fully absorbing something with a deep understanding. Many of our talks would lead to debates and sometimes full-blown arguments, with other inmates joining in on the conversations. A hot topic I remember having was about gangs. In the prison system 95% of the population is affiliated with gangs. Regardless of age or race, most people are in some sort of gang.

Growing up, I too used to try to align myself with gangs, but as I grew in maturity and wisdom, I've come to permanently cut off all ties and affiliations with such groups. I questioned Bad Wolf about how full-grown men can sit in prison in their 30's, 40s, and 50's run around and play gangster. Yet wonder why they can't figure life out or wonder why gang life is not prosperous one. Gangs are disorganized groups, with a lack of resources, lack of structure, and a lack of knowledge. They are going up against society. An organized government with unlimited resources, power, personnel, and intelligence. The negatives far out way the positives by a landslide. Everyone knows this to be true, but still choose to join an organization destined to fail.

I was curious to get Bad Wolf's opinion on what the root of the problem is. Once the root is identified, solutions are then able to take place. Bad Wolf responded to my question by saying, " glorification of street life through rap music, tv, and other media sources tend to play the role in developing the mentality that drug violence, breaking the law, and living a unrighteous life makes you "cool" and socially accepted by your peers. Therefore, making gang affiliation seem appeasing."

I can attest to this observation. Rap music and urban culture played a major role in me being allured by the street life, and gang affiliation. Even though I was not a "gang member", affiliating with such groups was just as destructive and harmful.

This conversation attracted others to join in. An inmate who goes by "War Eagle"-a member of the Native American Gang "Savage Boyz", said "Some people are just born into the lifestyle and don't know anything different; my father is from Savage Boyz and raised me to follow his footsteps. When your whole family embraces this lifestyle, it would be unnatural for me to stray from the path they laid out for me." I can understand this aspect and there are many that share this narrative. This is how I responded with hopes of giving him a different way of viewing things "I can understand what you're saying, because at the end of the day my family's influence is what makes me take the stand I'm taking. The only difference is the lifestyle my family wants to live and the one I'm choosing to live by is a righteous, prosperous lifestyle, that won't lead me doing time. If going to prison is something that you don't want to do, and want to avoid at all cost, then anything that has the chance to put you in that situation has to be examined, evaluated, and scrutinized to determine if you think it's worth the chance or not. I'm pretty sure your family won't disown you for choosing to do the righteous. Even if they did, it's all about how you want to live your life."

War Eagle's cellmate" Lil Bear" offered an explanation of his own to answer why gang affiliation is so prevalent. He said "When you had homeboys, family, etc. that have lost their lives to this life and you have been a part of a brotherhood for so long, you gain an undying loyalty to it. Something that is simply hard to shake even if you have the desire to."

This response silenced me for a while. At the time I didn't know how to retort back to what he shared with me. I couldn't discover what he said because that is, in my opinion, one of the main reasons people hang on to gangs. The ones who are in it or around it for image or reputation quickly flee when things take a turn for the worst- like me. However, the people who have that lifelong commitment and loyalty that is so strong they are willing to die for the cause have a deeper and more intimate attachment that has to be examined closer to find the root and come to truth.

I never had friends or people I loved lose their lives to gang violence, so I couldn't relate to what Lil Bear told me. But because our conversation was a building process and not just a trivial debut, I pondered on what he told me through the night and meditated on an answer to this real problem. I was fully confident there was an answer because "Mind Is the Master " convinced me completely that living righteous is the only way to happiness and propensity. And everyone has equal access to this. Being in prison doesn't bring happiness, therefore one must stay out. Gang activity leads to prison, so one must abstain from any membership of unlawful factions.

I knew these things to be true but wanted to try and convince others on the vent as well. They all had the desire to leave prison and stay out. This is the reason I even deemed it necessary to try to help because I know what it's like to lead a destructive life and want out but not have the courage, determination or positive push to allow for this to happen.

The next morning, I got on the vent to holler at Lil Bear and pick up things up from the day before. This is what I said to him, "What's up Lil Bear. I thought about what you told me last night and couldn't respond to it then. I had to sleep on it and give it more insight. I can see why someone will feel an obligation to give his loyalties towards a cause that his loved ones gave their lives for. Here is a way you can honor your fallen comrades and still honor yourself. A certified win, win case scenario. With the understanding that losing your life to gang violence is senseless and avoidable, don't let their deaths be in vain by not learning that lesson thus, setting yourself up for the same demise. You can look at it like they made the sacrifice to save you. By learning from their experience, you can avoid a similar fate. Most likely, that is what they would want if they had the opportunity to tell you furthermore, if you want to do a justice for your homeboys put yourself in a position which enables you to provide aid, assistance, and relief to their families. There nothing you can do for anybody from a prison cell. Make a real come back and become successful. Absolutely no one who absolutely loves you will rather you self-destruct than to become successful.

I'm not sure if Lil Bear was fully convinced of the logic I tried to give, but he heard me out and at least considered that I had a valid point.

This was a major step, because the shed of doubt has been planted and can now grow to yield positive results. That's how it happened for me. Change does not take place instantaneously it takes daily progress, but the starting point is definitely the realization of error and the willingness to correct it!

Simba's cellmate "Choose Up" got on the vent and offered another common contributor to the recidivism rate. He said "Besides gangs, I can see that most crimes are money motivated. The lack money, or the lack of knowledge to obtain the desired amount legally is one of the main issues. "

This observation piqued my curiosity, being that I fell into the category as well. I wanted to hear him all the way out. The problem was identified now I wanted to hear what he felt the solution could be.

He continued saying, "There is no simple one step solution. If we are talking about changing more than ourselves, it will have to start with us. No one will listen to someone who isn't implementing his own advice. We would have to get out and really explore legal business. Most of us are just afraid of it because it is a new territory we've never tried before. Fear of the unknown is why a lot of people don't explore new terrain. Entrepreneurship is a realistic way to gain that financial freedom that we all desire to have. No formal education is needed, and you can start a small business with little and sometimes even no funds. A solid support system will make achieving this easier, but even if one is not there, we must have the courage to try it anyway. What's the worst that can happen? Failure is the only possible negative result that can happen. I suggest keeping a job on the side, so you never fall completely off. What will be the worst outcome in trying illegal business? We all are too familiar with the answer to that question. That being said, we have nothing to lose. The best way to be ready for the streets is to start research now. You all have family, have them do research on small startup businesses and get as much information as you can. Study it intensely and write down as many plans as you can think of on how you can get out and start a business. Once you successfully do this, you will then be in a position to teach others. They will be more receptive to your teachings because they can see for themselves you have a proven method. From there you network and build your business. Surround yourself and align yourself with other business people. Once you are at a certain point, you can give back by helping fund, teach, and mentor other people. So, they can avoid incarceration, thinking their only route to money is by doing something illegal. Show others how easy and rewarding getting legal money can be.

This answer from "Choose Up" left no doubt in my mind what I had to do. He, without reading "Millionaire Prisoner" validated a lot of the same views that Josh Kruger and Mike Enemigo have.

My celly " Bobby Hill" elaborated even more to what Choose Up said, by saying, "What you said is true Choose Up, but before you can even get to that point you have to be willing to work hard, remain humble, and be patient. When we get out things won't always go according to plan or come as expected. There will be people out there who are doing better than us. Driving better cars, having better clothes, attracting beautiful women, the whole nine. We will be tempted to want to rush things to try to play catch up. Working hard and diligent is required but also accepting the fact that we will start from the bottom."

This was good insight from my celly. He usually doesn't partake in our conversations. I can only speculate that after realizing we have a genuine desire to change and lead successful lives, it inspired him to give his thoughts on the topic.

I was starting to see the difference our positive attitudes and thoughts were having on each other. If all you talk about is positive and legal endeavors, others are left with no choice in what they discuss with you because then they know you won't entertain frivolous, counter-productive chatter. I've had enough of the negativity and will rather go mute than to allow negative talk to take place in my life.

There have been times when debates will boil to become heated arguments, with inmates vowing not to speak to each other again. When I sensed a conversation take a turn into an argument, I will leave the vent all together with no warning. My only purpose to talk on the vent is to build and not destroy. Besides, it takes at least two to have an argument. I don't care about being right or having the last word. The only goal I have is to better myself. I looked at these conversations through the vent to be practice for me and a test to my commitment for a true change.

Some may think that a change to do right is an easy thing to do, or not as a challenge as some make it to be. If that's the case, why are so many incarcerated? I've met very few people who are indifferent to being in prison. Most inmates will rather not be confined. They want to live a better-quality life and also have the desire to change.

I say this to assert that change is not an easy feat. Especially when you've spent most of your life living, breathing, thinking, and conducting yourself in a certain way.

In my case, I must deprogram fifteen years of poor choices, poor thoughts, and poor habits all within a year before I go home to increase my chances of living the life I yearn to live. Not only just to stay free, but to also feel spiritually and emotionally satisfied.

Desire alone won't give me the results I expect. I've tried that already, I must drastically take action, and do whatever is necessary to make righteous thought and behavior a habitual occurrence.

My talks on the vent, daily studies, mediations, prayers, vigilant awareness, and family support area all key elements that allowed me to finally become the man I was destined to be.

Brandon
The Vent Talks

Over the years of me being incarcerated I've had my fair share of conversations through the vent. Considering my previous mind state a lot of these conversations happened to be frivolous and meaningless. Through my evolution I slowly started to change my attitude towards life and continued to perfect myself so naturally my thought pattern changed, thus my conversations.

Maturing mentally and spiritually allowed me to redirect my focus from being a child to becoming a strong, dependable man. I realized that a lot of the conversations I held were unproductive. I would try and relate too people and level with them on topics that didn't really hold weight with me, so I equate this to being fake. You might have heard of the saying "fake it 'til you make it" well, that's what I was doing faking the funk until I made a conscious decision to quit entertaining the negativity.

With this change came another obstacle. Self-righteousness. As I started having more intellectual dialogues, I realized that I began coming off as a know it all. Projecting myself to be this perfect entity with no flaws, realizing this, I quickly corrected myself.

Now, everyone many are not on the path of righteousness, but I commend those who are. Not only is it a strenuous process that requires vigilance and dedication, but it is also one of the positivity and reward, not only for those traveling this road, but for those met along the way as well. There is a ripple effect that takes place, activating and encouraging those who once upon a time didn't consciously seek righteousness to evaluate themselves and embrace the higher self within. During this, the ripple effect continues to evolve until it becomes a tsunami affecting a great many pushing them to become better.

During this time in the Intensive Supervision Unit, I help many talks with the people in the vents. The talks ranged from typical prison talk as in woman, prison, politics, grievance processes, prison operations; to creation of the universe, religion, morals and becoming righteous. I've shared war stories, I've had heated arguments, I've laughed and even shed tears over the vent. Ultimately, I've had life changing experiences that rocked me into the man I am currently through the vent.

Out of all these conversations though, some help gravity that pulled me back down to Earth and these are the talks we're going to break down.

The first of those I want to discuss is that typical prison operations. The not so good guys versus the bad guys. I say not so good guys referring to the staff. Why? You may ask. The answer is because these "civilians" have a set of rules they should adhere to but in reality, they break these rules every day without consequence, but in turn punish us for every little infraction. True hypocrisy. This is highly evident, especially in ISU. One wrong move and you can expect a write up.

As I went about day to day, doing the typical things of the prison life, these are the things I dwelled on heavily. Meditating on the fact that humans will be humans and no one's perfect, I developed an understanding: People will continue in the behavioral pattern that they are accustomed to if left unchecked.

One day I happened to be talking to my celly abut this matter. I mentioned to him my observation and of course it was met opposition. I told him that if we all stood together as a unit, we would see a change and it would produce a more comfortable environment. He responded that it wouldn't and proceeded to brush me off as crazy. I tried to defend my hypothesis but was quickly over-ruled by my peers and just as they thought my idea was irrational, I too believed they were completely illogical.

My defense consisted of me relaying facts. The main point I was making was the grievance process. Though I believe its length, I also believe if used properly it will be effective. One of the people on the vent replied it was against his by-laws to put in paperwork on the staff because it was considered snitching. This came in itself blew my mind; I wouldn't believe he possessed the audacity to reveal this to me. To me that was blasphemy. Then, to make it worse it was confounded when another inmate added his thoughts to the conversation. His input was this, "I've been in the pen for 15 years and I've never seen a grievance work". I asked him a simple question: "Have you ever tried it?" as I suspected he answered "no".

Now, I'm not trying to play the right and wrong game, because like I said my theory was exactly that, a theory. But, using my ability to reason I concluded that the point wasn't worth defending anymore. The grievance procedure is available for the rectification of any problems you may encounter. If you use it accordingly, you will have success. Granted, we are not playing a fair game and sometimes, we have to go the extra mile and put in extra work to get the results we want. This here is where most fall short. First of all, a large majority of the prison population doesn't use this tool, they would rather buck the system and act out, instead of approaching the situation in a calm and professional manner resulting in self destruction. With this proves you won't even learn the valuable lesson of self-control, resulting in a continuous downward spiral.

Like I said earlier the game isn't fair and I witnessed this on the two times I filled grievances. They were both for the same issue and looking at the truth, they were both denied because of my ignorance and negligence. But don't get me but don't give me wrong, there was definitely foul play going on. You may be wondering what I'm speaking of. Let me explain. The first time I put my grievance in, and I didn't attach a form that was needed in order for my agreements to be processed. Realizing this I quickly corrected my mistake and sent the quick for the back to be reviewed. I waited a couple weeks in suspense, and when I got the grievances back, they were both denied for various reasons. One being filling out the grievance on an improper grievance form. Now, this is where the scandal takes place. The grievance forms provided by the staff where the grievance forms that were out of date and therefore unexcepted. That was the first part, but the kicker is yet to come this is what got me. Like I said I honestly make a mistake and quickly try to correct it. And doing this was my downfall. When I received the paperwork back it came with two denial forms, one for each grievance this is how they played me: getting both grievances back at the same time; one saying I needed to correct the previous issues; the other saying due to my continued failure I am out of time. If I got both grievances back at the same time how would I be able to correct my mistakes. I couldn't! So, they got me. Technicalities can either save you or destroy you. Luckily, they save me. Yes, I lost a bad if I didn't lose the war. Reviewing the paperwork, I received, I figured out how they bamboozled me and prepare myself for my next battle.

Eventually, I was removed from that situation and placed in another cell which meant another event and new "vent friends". The conversations on this event were a little more fruitful. I shared my ideas and theories with this group and on a lot of things we concurred, but a lot of things ended up in hurt feelings and ill temper's. When I shared my theory of sticking together and filling paperwork to my surprise the people on the vent agreed. This encourage me to gather up communication for the next fight I see myself and with the "not so good guys".

Now, I can think back on a couple conversations on the vent that got heated to the point of name calling and threats, eventually leading to disassociation. One of these talks were so trivial so I look back on it I am disappointed in myself for even entertaining it and allowing it to escalate into a full-blown verbal altercation. The argument was over snakes. Yeah, legless reptiles that won't ever benefit me unless I found myself in the snake selling business which I don't see happening anytime soon. The actual subject was water moccasins eating fish and boa constrictor snakes eating live pray.

So, I began recounting a time where I went fishing with a buddy of mine. We took a 2-3-hour trip to the lake stopping along the way to buy some bait, minnows, worms, and some layers. When we got there, we kick back and finished off the deck. I had my minnows in a water key to allow them to have freshwater, they remain caves as well. We're going to retrieve one of these little guys. I saw a large snake swimming towards my minnows and what I believe to be as an attempt to eat them. Once again, my logic was met with radical. I believe the snake to be a water moccasin and this was the point I argued. To further my point, I told the "prosecutor" that I, on another fishing expedition seen an actual snake with a perch in its mouth. He began to ask how it is possible for a snake to eat a fish in the water. I had no answer. All I could say was the things I witness. Basically, the same thing happened with the snake eating live animals. I witnessed in high school my Science teacher snake ate a mouse. He hit it, constricted it to the point of an immobility then while it was still kicking, ingested it. I was then called multiple dumb asses and stupid asses and blah, blah, blah. Eventually the guy called his girlfriend, and she confirmed my theory. Water moccasins eat fish and other snakes eat live animals. The conversation was frivolous, but I gained valuable insight from it. Quit arguing. Thus, began my journey of mastering the art of tact. Knowing when to shut up. I started practicing this and allow people to have the last word this resulted in may being able to understand that humility plays a huge role in the success. With this knowledge I begin coming off less as a know it all and began to lead by example.

More chats followed and I began to grow less and less entertaining. Considering the fact that the majority of the conversations were largely based off of opinions, it occurred to me that even allowing the potential argument was not among my best interest.

The same person I had to snag debate with had a habit of getting on the vent and talking about maturity and enjoying ridiculing and making jokes about me. I eventually, after much practice developed a talent I like to refer to as "leaving orbit." Now before you runoff and think I went down the deep end hear me out. The living orbit technique is performed as follows: somebody calls my name, I answer it and if they begin talking about nonsense I immediately quit responding and continue my business that I was attending to before they decided to try and bring me to a bad place mentally, thus leaving their sphere after that and returning to my peaceful state. Far out? I told you I was a hippie! Don't judge me.

These conversations the good, bad, and ugly all played a role in helping me become more conscious of myself. Since we're on the topic of far out and leaving orbit I must go into the talks about the universe. Of course, all of this was speculative, so these were some of the more painless talks we held.

My view on this matter was that the universe is built upon scientific and mathematical principles and just as there are multiple numbers, I believe that there are multiple dimensions and universes. I'm not going to go in depth and risk confusing you but like I said before all of it is speculative anyways. Other inmates held her own ideas, one was kind of interesting and referred to the universe as just a part of another unfathomable entity. Kind of like a cell to an organism. Though we can fathom a cell, the cell can't fathom us. It was a cool perspective to hear. It is always doped to examine other people's thoughts on the cosmos. Once again though, I learned to humble myself. I don't know everything, and the more I learn the better I can become as a man.

On the vent we've had music sessions, jamming out all night. I know the neighbors wanted us to go to sleep. But ultimately, the vent was my salvation. It allowed me to examine myself and learn from others leading me to become the best person I can be. I can honestly say my attitude towards myself and life has greatly changed all because I have these vent talks.

If it wasn't for the vent, I wouldn't have ever met Chris, I wouldn't have ever received the Mind is the Master Book, and the confirmations that came with it. When you're in sync with God and his creation, the universe truly become unstoppable. This all starts with seeking righteousness and submitting to the greater good.

My journey just so happens to leave me to the vent. And guess what? It doesn't end here. I have a lot more life to live and at this pace it looks to be a very prosperous one! I remember telling the mother of my son about the girls in the vent, she tried to play the crazy card on me and asked me if they were real. Oh, the irony.

Chapter 10

Christopher

Laughing in the Face of Circumstances

Serving time in prison has been the most humbling experience I ever endured. I've lost my freedom, dignity, pride, and respect. On a constant basis I've faced adversity and many challenges. Unlike having the ability to run from my problems, like I would in the free world, I've had to figure out how to deal with my issues head on.

The hardest times were at the beginning of my sentence. I had a hard reality check, that no one is going to make things easy for me. No one cares about you being in prison. Sympathy and empathy were left at home. As much as my family supported me and helped me along the way, I still had to walk this path alone.

I've had to learn through trial and error how to handle the various obstacles presented to me. Anger and violence did nothing for me but cause self-destruction and misery. One of the most valuable lessons I've learned is that most issues can be avoided, if you take the proactive approach rather than just being reactive to every situation.

I view your peace of mind as your "power". When you let someone disturb this you are giving them your power. The trick that I use to help me conquer every situation dealing with people is figuring out how to maintain my power. Every interaction you have with someone has a level of energy to it. Without this energy there would be no encounter. Any potential altercation that may arise can either escalate or deescalate depending on whether you add energy to the situation or take it away. The more you can take the energy from the situation, the more likely you'll maintain your power.

Laughter has been a great asset to me. The ability to minimize a situation by laughing it off, whether in your mind or out loud, has been one of my effective tactics in maintaining my power. There are many challenges that I've had to deal with on a regular basis. The more capable I was at laughing them off, the better my time got and the more peace at mind I was able to retain-My power.

CO's, inmates, women, friends, and facility operations are a few sources that I can trace most of my problems stemming from. CO's in my experience have been the most challenging to deal with. Not because I have an issue with authority or following the rules. The biggest adjustment was learning how to deal with how they treat you. Being that they are in a position of higher power, have authority, and are law abiding citizens doing their jobs, I had expectations of them. I expected them to conduct themselves as professionals, be fair, and do their jobs efficiently. Those expectations were miserably failed. My experiences showed me that CO's have the tendency to stereotype inmates, disrespect inmates, and carry a superior attitude towards inmates. Not all of the corrections officers are guilty of these actions, but a majority of them are. I have been accused of being a gang member repeatedly, even though I have admittedly denied such affiliations. I have been talked down to, as if I possess no intelligence. I've also heard CO's openly disregard inmate's safety and act no better than the criminals they get paid to watch.

After watching the CO's closely, trying to gain an understanding of why most of them conduct themselves certain ways, I've noticed a few things. They work a highly stressful job and deal with ignorance, disrespect, abuse, and other negative elements on a daily basis.

I began to easily understand how the CO's would act the way they do. Not saying that it is right, but from a realistic standpoint, it would be farfetched to expect someone who is overworked, underpaid, abused, disrespected, and unappreciated to display above par professionalism at all times. That is an unrealistic expectation to have on the average person. It takes special people who enjoy what they do and are dedicated to their career to maintain the standard of professionalism on a consistent basis. I've only seen a few of these types of CO's. The average CO's attitude is of the former not the latter.

Overtime I've figured out how to conduct myself towards the CO's to get the treatment I expected to get.

I made it a point to do the exact opposite of what they expected me to do. I wore all of my clothes fitted and didn't sag. I stopped using slang and vulgar language. I expanded my vocabulary to give me a more eloquent speech. I also gave them respect and went out of my way to greet or compliment them.

I did all these things to show the CO's I demanded respect. I don't want to be treated like a common criminal or an illiterate fool. At first, it was a form of rebellion by being the opposite of what they expected out of me. I was able to laugh when I could hear their reaction to me acting like a civilized human being. My intention at the beginning was only to prove to them that just because I'm incarcerated, doesn't make me an animal to be treated like a classless fool. However, as time went on and I continued to carry myself professionally towards the CO's, I started to notice that they would mirror my actions. They started addressing me with more respect, they would treat me a little kinder and it got to the point where we would even carry on with small talk. I finally started to feel like my respect was being restored.

I also learned several valuable lessons with the exercises I used towards the CO's. One, they are human, and they will treat you the way you treat them or yourself. Two, if you act and talk a certain way, you can't be surprised when people treat you a certain way.

The reality is if you want to maintain your power, dignity, and self-respect, you must carry yourself like it at all times.

The second most challenging group of people I've learned to deal with is the inmates. Other offenders can make your time extremely stressful if you let them down by not knowing how to deal with them.

While reading "Mind is the Master", I came across this passage and it gave me tremendous strength. "Within the sphere of his own mind man has all power, but in the sphere of other minds and outside things, his power is extremely limited. He can command his own mind, but he cannot command the mind of others. He can choose what he shall think, but he cannot control the weather as he wills, but he can control his mind, and decide what his mental attitude toward the weather shall be." This gave me insight and I applied this lesson immediately. I am on the journey of trying to evolve and become a better person and go home. Others don't have the same aspirations; therefore, we never see eye to eye. I've already been through the phase of living like a typical prisoner and decided that's not what I wanted. I strive to be the best person I can be morally, spiritual, and intellectually.

I applied my tactic of minimizing what others had to say about me in order to reduce any potential conflicts. In my head I would say "they're not talking about nothing" and laugh off whatever folly they may speak. Maintaining my power and thus living in peace and solitude. The attitude I had to adopt was not to care about what anyone had to say, because I knew what path I was on and would travel it alone.

Overtime I've noticed the number of confrontations I would have was substantially reduced. The power of laughter has helped me on numerous occasions. Taking everything too seriously was not doing any justice for me.

Another area where I had to apply laughter to help me through, was dealing with a woman I was in a relationship with. Maintaining a relationship while being incarcerated is extremely difficult and if you're not mature or dedicated enough to the relationship, it will not work. Because I learned this lesson too late, I was unable to salvage my relationship. I did, however, learn to laugh things off and remain humble, patient, and positive. This allowed me to maintain friendships with women without complications of being committed to an exclusive relationship.

Being incarcerated, you are subject to many things that are beyond your control. The only thing we can truly control is ourselves and how we respond to the circumstances. If I stressed out every time something did not go my way, I would go insane. It almost happened until I discovered the power of laughter.

Brandon

Laughing in the Face of Circumstances

I f it wasn't for laughter, the vent would have been irrelevant; it wouldn't have helped me at all. Because all the profound revelations were so real and raw, if I wasn't able to laugh it off, I knew for certain I wouldn't be able to contain the pain that came with the truth. I embraced it though and laughed at my folly in my previous mistakes because when I look back it was really a Goof Troop. The idiotic things I did burned bridges and commenced a series of unfortunate events.

Back then I couldn't break the pattern. I felt like it was bad luck, but really it was a lack of motivation and resources that led me to committing petty crimes. I never did anything hideous but yet I sit here and continue to serve a 15-year sentence. Without a sense of humor, I would have never made the conscious decision to seek change. I would be in the same situation I found myself in previous to my Great Awakening.

So yeah, I had to employ great resource laughter in order to make it through my ordeals. Sometimes I just sit and reminisce about the good ol' times, where I possessed no care in the world and no responsibilities. When I kicked it with my friends smoked weed and stayed out late. Like Khalid I was young, wild, and free. I laugh at all the crazy things I used to do, and I also shun them. I made plenty

184

of mistakes and definitely paid for the lessons I've learned. Without laughter, I may not have been able to gain the understanding that was necessary to apply the wisdom obtained. So, for this I am truly thankful, and truly blessed. To have been able to rise from the ashes and recover what life I have left.

Being in prison is a life-changing experience. Imagine being a young man, formerly gang involved, different outcast and looking for a way out. You find yourself surrounded by a pit of vipers, ready to bite you at every step you take to remove yourself from their environment. You must proceed with caution because any step could be your last if careless.

In order to survive, I had to embrace the situation I found myself in. The whole thing is really a parody. There is no other way to describe it. The story behind a man I am today is priceless. The goofy things I used to do, my foolish court jester mentality, the ironic places. I found myself in. Yeah, it's a story for the books all right.

If I wasn't able to make fun of myself, I would've probably been dead right now or truly crazy! But it's the triumph that's truly comedic. The joke is no longer on me though. I was at such a low place, exhausted spiritually devoid of self-respect and lacking motivation. Now I sit here a reformed man. Strong, intelligent, and driven. I have done a full 180° and placed myself on top of the world, where I should've been a long time ago.

Seeking righteousness enables me to wholly entertain myself; not at the expense of others but being able to look at my shortcomings, laugh at them and correct them.

When I talk about laughing at myself though it's not just a ha, ha funny, it's also a scoffing funny, like I can't believe I sucked this low funny. This is the only way I could rationalize the extreme disposition I advertently put myself in.

It was either one of two options: laugh or cry. I chose the former, though sometimes the latter was unavoidable. My theory was this: I dug this whole so, I can climb my way out of it no matter how long it took or how hard, I will get it done. And no, I'm not going to blame anyone for my predicament it all started with me. So no, I'm not going to expect anyone to help me. I'll do it myself if I have to. And I'll do it with a smile on my face and a song in my head. But don't get me wrong. All help is welcome. I refuse to burn any bridges by being foolish and not accepting people's kindness. I believe stop deprecating humor is healing though. It provides an outlet to brush things off that you can't change. If you can do this, you're a step ahead of the people who would choose to ridicule you. It really is an armor that allows you to deflect all the negativity that would thus be projected by peers.

I like to look at it like self-administering a poison in order to build a tolerance. You slowly and carefully strengthen your immunity dose by dose, ultimately resulting in you becoming impervious! This technique has assisted me and other people I've witnessed, laugh off their insecurities and make light where there would otherwise be darkness. I admire the people who are able to do this and divert the bullets of the slanderer. This is a display of true strength and beauty at its finest!

Now being able to listen to desensitize the fact that I am in the pen on a bogus charge is just the beginning. There are multiple things in here that can ruin a day if allowed to. One of these things happens to be the "Almighty staff." These people do whatever they want to, and act like it's OK. As I sit here right now, I just put another grievance in because they tried to give me some melted ice cream. Petty, yeah, but if allowed to continue this is all the CO who was on duty knew he was wrong because he just sat and allowed my ice cream to melt in front of my door. I repeatedly asked for it to avail. When he finally gave it to me it was a milkshake. I immediately refused it and told him to call the canteen personnel. He told me no to this as well. I hounded him the whole day about it, again to no avail. I didn't allow it to ruffle my feathers, no. Instead I submitted a request to staff and began a grievance process. I saved my receipt to prove I purchased the ice cream; I waited for two weeks and finally received the request to staff back. You remember earlier when I spoke about the grievance process to the staff abusing it, well once again I was shamed. The request I got back, to my expectations, said some crazy stuff. It said after recovering the cameras she didn't see me refuse the ice cream. Knowing I did, receiving the response was preposterous. But considering my previous encounters with these people I was prepared for anything., I just continued the grievance process. I laughed it off, knowing I'm going to get the last laugh.

With a cool head and a sense of humor I would have been all out of my element, letting the situation control me. You can lock my body up, but you can't cage my mind.

Every day presents a problem in this world I live in and I'm sure it does in the real world as well. But here I'm isolated and I have dishonest people who are charged with the responsibility of overseeing me. It is a constant challenge but working to better myself I've developed a sense of humor about it all. These people will just classify you as a liar, a cheater, and a swindler without taking the time to get to know you, assuming because you're in prison you have to be immoral.

Personally, a lot of my mistakes didn't transpire from immorality but from ignorance. I believe a good two-year rehabilitation would have done the trick but instead, here I am.

I witness people getting into shouting matches with the staff, cursing back-and-forth. Just last night I watched an inmate and a CO cuss each other out. The CO stayed in front of his door and continued to argue with the inmate about the phone. I thought it was an unbelievable display of lack of self-control. It perplexes me how one in a position of authority could be flustered by someone trapped behind a door. Then it hit me. We all are just humans and we are all just trying to make it to see tomorrow.

I know a lot of things I've done have been being a young man in the penitentiary you are heavily pressured by your peers to join a gang and they are prevalent. Everywhere you go you hear somebody ripping' their set. You hear people hollering, people fighting, getting stabbed, recruiting. It's a nonstop flux of activity and the majority of it is positive.

The best thing you can do is stay to yourself and blend in. You have to take precautions not to stand out and make it seem like you're doing too much because the Lone wolf is defenseless against a pack unless he can out with them.

My remedy to this is to keep an open mind and not allow my emotions to cloud my judgment. I'm doing this and I am able to act accordingly to whatever situation I may find myself in. I allow myself to adapt, and the more I apply wisdom the better the outcomes are. After multiple fights and disagreements, I learned an invaluable lesson, the Wiseman is a master of tact and displays his eloquence in every scene he finds himself in and doesn't resort to violence when provoked but instead approaches the situation with a composed and understanding nature. This enables him to defuse the situation completely and also provides a sterling example how a man should compose himself.

Prisoners also often encounter loneliness. Everybody in this situation knows what it's like to be lonely. A lot of the time those you associate yourself with continue to live their life once you're once you become incarcerated. Out of sight out of mind. With that being said, some come to a realization that it's just them. They believe that they are all they have and develop a better attitude toward people in general. When I was in the world, I had a few friends who actually called friends. They were with me through the good times and the bad. I know if I needed them right now, they would help if it's within their reach. But being locked up and out of their immediate thoughts they will quickly forget about me, considering the fact that they have full lives of their own to live. So, who am I to be mad at them for not babying me and writing me when I want them to? They didn't put me in here, I did. So, understanding this fact I must act accordingly. I am a grown man who has made plenty of bad decisions in life based on a lack of knowledge, or my own ignorance in other words, but as I gain knowledge, I consciously choose to apply it. Yes, I do get lonely, sometimes it seems like people don't care about me, but this isn't the truth of the matter. People have things going on with themselves. Who is to say they aren't mad at me for leaving them in the world?

The people who help me understand this or my son and his mother. Though she was directly involved in me receiving this sentence she doesn't owe me anything, she's doing what she should be and that's raising my son. Previously I had the false notion that she was obligated to help me considering her role in the events leading me here. But I was wrong. It all started with me. She didn't force me to listen to her. I did willingly and pushed comes to shove and bam I'm here. Yeah, my rash decisions lead me to my current predicament, so there's no one to blame but myself. So, guess what? I would just laugh it off and work on me. If I was a better person when I was out, I bet more people would be willing to give some of their time to help, but I wasn't, and therefore, realizing this I must transfer myself and be the best man possible.

My time is limited here, and I must enjoy the few remaining days I have left. I refuse to be controlled by other people and their foolishness and insecurities. I choose to enjoy life and the people and things that come with it. Life is way too short to be bitter and negative. We are all one people and should act like it and help one another experience the joys of life. There are too many beautiful things to focus on to be concerned with the unattractive. And the more we understand the more beauty we will see in each other. We are one in the same so instead of fighting and becoming disgruntled, we should stand together and laugh in the face of the circumstances we all find ourselves in.

Chapter 11

Christopher

The Do's and Don'ts

My time in the phase program (the hole) became tranquil and serene. I felt an unwavering calm and peace in the midst of the storm. With a clear vision of where I was going in life and how I was going to get there, I no longer had anxiety or fear of what my future held.

I used to tell myself all the time that "I will die before I come back to prison". What depressed me the most was that I was not even confident that I could get out and stay out for good. The statistics scared me. The fact that eight of ten felons came back to prison, did little to build my confidence that I can be one of the lucky few who can escape this concrete tomb forever.

After I dedicated my life to being a righteous man, it became noticeably clear to me that "luck" had nothing to do with the outcome of my future. It has everything to do with myself and I have total control over what I think, how I react and what decisions I make.

It all comes to the do's and don'ts that we integrate into our lives. Everyone has their own set of do's and don'ts. I've come across this passage from James Allen entitled "The Righteous Man" and decided this is the person I shall become "The righteous man is invincible. No enemy can possibly overcome or confound him; and he needs no other protection than that of his own integrity and holiness. The righteous man, having nothing to hide committing no acts which require stealth, and harboring no thoughts and desires which he would not like others to know, is fearless and unashamed. His step is firm, his body upright, and his speech direct and without ambiguity. He looks everybody in the face. How can he fear anyone who wrongs none? How can he be ashamed before any who deceives none? And ceasing from all wrong he can never be wronged; ceasing from all deceit he can never be deceived. The righteous man, performing all his duties with scrupulous diligence, and living above sin, is invulnerable at every point. He who has slain the inward enemies of virtue can never be brought by any outward enemy; neither does he need to seek any protection against the righteousness being an all-sufficient protection. The unrighteous man is vulnerable at almost every point; living in his passions, the slave of prejudices, impulses, and ill-formed opinions, he is continually suffering (as he imagines) at the hands of others. The slanders, attacks, and accusations of others cause him great suffering because they have a basis of truth in himself: and not having protection of righteousness, he endeavors to justify and protect himself by resorting to retaliation and specious argument and even to subterfuge and deceit".

After reading, absorbing, and meditating on these wise words from James Allen, it became very obvious and plain what needed to be done. Excuses are useless and I cannot run from the truth because it was revealed to me for a reason. There is no reason to fear the suffering of a consequence stemming from an action you never committed. This made perfect sense to me. I just had to look at every aspect in my life and determine what was needed and what was not. All of the unlawful practices, immoral ways of thinking and behaving were not conducive to the lifestyle I want to live, so that falls under the don't category. I developed the habit of watching people's behavior and picking up the things they did and what the results would be because of their actions.

It was easier for me to watch and learn from other people. I think this was because I was able to watch people and see the absolute truth. With no prejudice or biased opinion.

I watched everyone from CO's, inmates, nurses, to the people on tv. This helped me in many ways. It allowed me to look at the world around me and witness reality without having my personal feelings influence my thoughts.

I was able to identify the self-destructive thoughts that enabled me to become incarcerated. Minimizing my actions, thinking that I wasn't doing as bad as my neighbor, so it's no big deal for me to illegally hustle. I can see how justifying an action of lifestyle in your mind will allow you to fully engage because you have tricked yourself into thinking it's alright. A delusional mind-frame is what I was in and now I must take full control of my mind. Controlling my thoughts is the biggest chance of success. My thoughts have direct relation to my actions.

Pure thoughts will result in pure action. It seems so simple, but it took me many, many years to finally arrive at this conclusion. The beauty I see in my particular situation is that I now know what I want to be in this world and how I want to live. I have one year left before I go home and plenty of time to work on myself from the top to the bottom. I don't want to just maintain my freedom and liberties. I want to become a better person and help contribute to society. If I can help the next person come out of spiritual hibernation, then I've done something worthwhile.

I realized in my journey there are many who wish to change their life around, but not too many have the guidance, knowledge, support, or strength to make the necessary changes. I myself, did not. I had help from my family and was blessed to come across James Allen's "Mind is the Master". So, I feel compelled to pass the wisdom forward and apply the teachings to my life. Also, thanks to Joshua Kruger and Mike Enemigo who showed me how to free my mind and think outside the box to generate money under any circumstance legally. This was a blessing that came from the sky. Just by having a positive conversation on the vent "Millionaire Prisoner" was revealed to me, thus changing my life forever.

195

Being the creature of my thoughts and universe showed me how much power that I truly have. So much time was wasted thinking that things were the way they were just because. Influence plays a major role in what people think and do. I see how I let the influence of culture, music, movies, and other people shape how I thought. Allowing others to control my thoughts is unacceptable. Retaining all power of thought is the most important thing a person can do when it comes to being master of his or her universe. I have been used to living, thinking, and behaving a certain way for so long I've decided I must start all the way over. Take it all the way to the drawing board. I'm already away from society, technology, and other worldly distractions. This will be the perfect opportunity to reinvent myself.

Brandon
The Do's and Don'ts

Navigate the treacherous roads we call life; we learn what to do and what not to do along the way. Well I can't speak for everyone, but with as many breakdowns and wrecks that I've experienced it eventually learned how to drive. Coming from a guy who used to run life's "red lights" and disregard life's "street signs" I finally learned it would be less costly if I just follow the rules. Yeah, sounds horribly boring, I know. No more pedal to the metal, no more high-speed chases, no more carefree living. But also, it comes with that is no more tickets and court dates. Growing up and maturing, I will gladly make the trade. It was fine when I was young, bucking the system, fighting the authorities, being an anarchist and rebel. But eventually it grows old. In and out of jail, losing good people that matter so much, being homeless; that life's not for me. I finally had to realize this and begin doing what's right!

What is right? One of my questions. Right to a matter of perspective but Webster's dictionary defines right as "Being in accordance with what is just good or proper." It has many definitions, but this is the one I want to focus on. To you a little deeper we have to look at the definition for just. Just means morally or legally right. Uhhuh! We finally got to it. When I speak of doing the right thing, I simply mean doing what is morally and legally right. Yeah, considering my background this is easier said than done. But with determination and motivation, it can be accomplished in no time.

After the last fender bender I found myself in, I finally decided enough is enough. I renounced my old ways and had to start anew.

I became more interested in the law-abiding citizens who live their life day to day without a single thought of the police depriving them of their freedom. I started imagining myself like them, going about life with a good attitude knowing I'm doing the right thing. Embodying this role, I felt my worries melt away, I envisioned myself enjoying my family and friends, supporting myself legally and being happy with my circumstances knowing where I came from. This drove me to the start vigorously searching for what is right.

And I began adopting the qualities of the people who were directly surrounding me that were on the "right" side of the law. That just happened to be the staff. Though I believe they break rules all the time, they were doing something I wasn't. Working. These people pay taxes, and they have a fixed income if they go to work to get paid. Just like that. If they perform at work, they can expect a promotion and get paid more. They don't have to worry about the employer not paying them. Why? Because it is an organized taxpaying entity that prides itself in being just such.

As I studied the staff, humbled myself and really became an impasse, I felt what they felt, and saw what they saw. I witnessed the daily struggles they had to overcome. I watched them come to work sick and tired and still they did their job. I began to admire these people. I may have spoken a bit harshly about them in earlier chapters, but I can't take away from the hard work they put in. Though I may disagree with some of their moral choices, they repeatedly do what is necessary in order to provide a life they want for themselves and their families if they have one.

This was just the beginning of me rerouting my life. With this change of course, I begin looking at the world from a perspective I never knew was possible for me. I begin seeing all the possibilities, not just the fact that I could hold a job, but I could do anything I put my mind too. I realize there was always a way in or a way out.

According to my circumstances I needed both a way in a way out. I needed a way into legitimate money and a way out of prison and the unproductive life I previously led. With this new view of life, it didn't take long to conjure up a way. Knowing this is what I wanted, I pondered on it day and night. I began running scenario after scenario through my mind trying to find a solution for my problem when it finally hit me. "Just do it." Is what I came up with. This isn't a Nike ad but that's the simplest way I can put it. Just get up and do it. The only things I needed were an able body and sound mind and I have both of these at my disposal.

I began plotting. I decided I was going to become legitimate and all endeavors and the book the "Millionaire Prisoner" helped compound my ideas. I took the knowledge that I already possessed, and with the things I already loved I came up with a plan. Just like I love to hustle illegally I would begin my legal hustle. Where there is supply, there is demand. And with my hustlers mentality I'm bound for success while doing the things I fancy. Now I can enjoy my life without the worry of getting busted. When I speak of legitimacy I'm talking about squeaky clean business, from contracts to lawyers. Jail? Ain't nobody got time for that, for real. I want to have a peaceful life and be able to provide for the people I care about the most.

Now, the things I have to do to break out of prison (metaphorically of course) are a little bit more complicated, but with the same mantra "Just do it," I know I can succeed.

It all starts again with doing what's morally and legally right. First of all, I must remain on my best behavior and embody the righteous man that I am. With the help of James Allen's books, I know exactly how to be this Righteous Man, therefore I am already free mentally and spiritually but it's the physical part that needs work. So, I maintain an optimistic attitude and approach, while trying to Houdini out of these handcuffs.

Where there's a will, there's a way. We all have heard this cliché, but there definitely is some truth that resonates with it. With an iron will nothing is too far out of reach but dedication to a task we can accomplish anything. With this knowledge, I know exactly what to do and that's to exploit every resource.

So, I am currently exploring all options and avenues in order to set an example for those that follow me. Prison is a place for the man who has found himself and wants to do good in life. Neither is any other negative predicament that one may find him/ herself in. Get out! We deserve to live our best lives and enjoy every second of it. We do this by doing what's righteous. When I say righteous, I don't mean overly religious, I mean being a person of integrity and knowing your value in the order of life. Whatever you may believe, I believe it's up to you. The only thing that classifies you as wrong or right is society's norms. I've searched and meditated on this subject and came up with the conclusion that there is no right or wrong in nature, except when you observe the higher realms of intelligence that is so rightly ours, the human beings. We literally have a written law and moral code and depending on which you follow the circumstances differ. In some cases, the written law clashes with the moral code of religion. To each his own, I believe that the best moral code for me to follow is the one of truth, love, and peace. With this view on life I believe I can't lose.

Reteaching myself how to drive I didn't just need to focus on the things to do but also the things not to do. One of these things happens to be the people I associate myself with. Growing up a

Christian there was one scripture that my mom kept reminding me of and that's "Bad associations spoil useful habits." The gravity of this scripture didn't sink in until just recently. It finally hit me how true those few words rang. When I realize the people, I associate myself with didn't share the same values in life I quickly begin changing up.

Some people say they will never change. It's sad to hear this because a universal truth is that stagnation means death. With this knowledge I am constantly seeking change for the better. If this means being alienated, so be it, ET.

I have never been one to follow the trends and don't plan on starting but it's really hard to isolate y

elf and be a loner by choice but it's necessary in this place I currently live in. If I want to evolve into the man I can be at the peak of my potential, I must choose to walk that lonely road. I can't keep doing the things that lead me to prison and entertaining bad associates is one of these things.

The big heart person that wants to help everybody still exists, but I have to learn the art of finesse. I can't help anybody if I don't have any resources. But the more resourceful I become the more capable I'll be to assist my followers. I can't keep squandering my blessings. That would be counter-productive, resulting in me driving in reverse. And this leaves me with the second "Don't, don't make unwise choices." Not making unwise choices is applicable to self-

spheres of life. From property to time. Everything must be done wisely.

I can't lie, I used to take things for granted. The small things and the large. I used to be completely indifferent to the majority of my circumstances. I didn't value the little time I had on Earth, I didn't value my family, my teachers, or friends. I just walk through life with the "it is what it is" attitude I formally mentioned. This attitude was the death of me. I found myself without the least bit of self-respect. I was just a tumbleweed getting blown about by the hot desert wind, not caring about where I landed. That was a story of my life until I recently decided to take control.

I began making wiser decisions. I begin valuing the little things. Life is precious, and with the aesthetic view it becomes blissful.

So, no I can't look at people and get mad. I can look at them with an understanding nature and hopefully indirectly teach them a lesson in patience. Life is too short to grovel and be depressed. So, I choose to love myself. With the unselfish love of self, I can easily love everyone else. I know I wasn't always this person. Though I didn't realize it, I was selfish and pretentious. I was heavily flawed, and my past reflects this. I was lost in the sauce and didn't really understand life. But I continued to seek truth and eventually led myself to the paradise of peace. It wasn't an easy task, referring back to the deriving metaphor I had my fair share of wrecks. I learned what to do and what not to do while traveling these beautiful but dangerous roads. But the last little wreck I found myself in resulted in death of the old man, which brought me to the point I find myself in now. The Reincarnation!

Chapter 12

Christopher

Reincarnation

With the understanding that who you are on the inside is a direct reflection of what your outer world is, you are your world. With the ability to change your inner thoughts at will, you are able to change your outer world at will. No one is subject to have a fixed mindset. Thus, having a fixed life. We all have the ability to change our mindset and course of life at any moment of our choosing.

I no longer wasted to just look at the next person and admire their positive characteristics and admire the life that they have created for themselves, with the hopeless thought that I cannot acquire the same attributes for myself. It was time for me to become the man I wanted to be, and not just sit on the sidelines and watch others living to their fullest potential without me doing the same thing. Desire without action is counterproductive in gaining the expected result.

The timing was perfect for me to do a complex re-invention of myself with no distractions or outside influences. I am already isolated from society and being that I am in phases I am now isolated within the prison from other inmates. Total isolation gave me the space and peace at mind to allow me to give a legitimate try.

205

Not sure of how to exactly start the process, I meditated for a few days and just pondered, "how can I do a complete change of myself from within?"

The first step I decided was to get two sheets of paper. On one I listed all of the qualities I have currently that I like on one side of the paper, and on the other side I listed all of the qualities that I want to acquire. On the other sheet of paper, I listed all of the vices, I wanted to rid myself of.

I needed to see everything on paper to make it tangible and real to me. The traits that I want to acquire were peace, patience, eloquence, happiness, gentleness, sincerity, and thoughtfulness. I looked at the list daily and meditated on the words. During my meditation, I envisioned the action behind the words "What do these words look like in action?" I would ask myself for example, I meditated on the word patience. When I wondered how that looked in real life. I thought of Barack Obama. I envisioned all the adversaries he encountered and how he always seemed in total control no matter what situation arose. I studied every detail down to the mannerisms and guessing what he might have been thinking in his head during times he's repeatedly been tested.

I started to feel progress, so I continued this exercise with the entire list that I compiled. Every trait that I did not like and wanted to get rid of was also written down and studied. I trained my mind to be constantly aware of my thoughts so that any time negativity would enter my mind I could redirect my thoughts.

This was no easy feat. So many thoughts come across your mind on a daily basis, so you have to constantly monitor what it is that you dwell on. I have not perfected this practice; however, I see tremendous growth and progress. Since I've attempted this practice, I've been thinking on a completely different level that I never reached before. It also gets easier the more I practice. The art of training my mind and thoughts when I think about who it is, I want to be in life to my family, friends, and everyone else, I picture myself in full detail. Everything from appearance, speech, actions, and intentions. Positivity is the impact I want to leave on anyone who encounters me.

Anything that does not align with my goals must be discarded. I have to let everything go that does not meet the new standards I've set for myself.

I want to be a reliable noble man who carries himself with dignity and treats others well. I want to be a good man that can impact the lives of others and still have a good time and enjoy life. Easy going and laid back are qualities I value. I used to take trivial things too seriously and I've experienced now how much energy it drains and how much time it wasted.

Perfection is viewed as a pentacle that humans are not able to reach. I've come to form the opinion that such a statement is an excuse. Have you ever heard someone say "Well, I'm just a human being and we make mistakes"? This is a way people justify committing actions they know are wrong. It's an easy way of minimizing and dismissing subpar behavior. Granted, we are humans and we indeed make mistakes but, if one strives for perfection and of course falls short, you will still be way better off and surpass the person who does not even strive for a level of perfection.

Evolution is life. One that lives in a world of stagnation is dead. Even if I take steps only one at a time, I can look back after a certain amount of time and recognize that I have in fact made progress from the starting point.

Like a snake who needs his old skin, I have shed the old bad habits and ways of the past. At first, it felt unnatural for me to completely change myself as if I were somehow "faking it". This feeling almost discouraged me from the path I was on because it felt that I was not truly getting anywhere, that instead I was "faking" my growth and just being delusional. This is a false and dangerous way of thinking. Self-doubt is one of the main barriers that keeps one from living up to their greatest potential.

In a way, to make a change in your life you do have to put on an "act". It requires action and expended energy to make things happen. Every single thing in life requires some form of action in order for that particular thing to exist. There would be no movies without actors.

Beyoncé may have sung in one of her songs "I woke up like this!" but I guarantee she put in work before she went to sleep! When I was out in the community, I never got the impression that people thought I was a gang banger or an illiterate fool. I was never treated that way until I got incarcerated. After experiencing treatment like that from CO's, I became very aware that how you present yourself carries much weight on how people view and treat you. Once I made the necessary adjustment to myself to establish that I wanted respect, I obtained the desired result. I've received positive results so I continued to do what I knew would give me the results I expected. I try to minimize slang in my speech and use more professional words. I decided to go with the clean-cut look and dress without sagging. I want to be treated like a professional so I know I must exude professionalism.

Sure, I enjoy urban culture and like the style. I can still express my taste and individualism the way I want. I am now just more aware of my surroundings and realize there is a time and place for everything. Selling myself short intellectually is never ok and something I'll never do again. There is no such thing as talking "black" or speaking "white". There is only eloquent speech or not. You can either use words effectively to convey your thoughts or not. I will never "dumb down" my speech to converse with peers, family, or friends again. That is saying in my opinion, one or two things either I am underestimating my peers, family, or friend's comprehension skills, or I don't respect myself enough to carry myself like a mature intelligent adult. Both scenarios don't sit well with me, so I chose to change it.

It used to make me feel uncomfortable to try and speak proper, because I knew I would be ridiculed for "trying to act like I'm smarter than other people". I never agreed with this sentiment because being the best you can be has nothing to do with minimizing or belittling the next person. I've come to realize anyone who processes it that way just has insecurities within themselves. No one should have to dim their own light in order to make others feel comfortable to shine.

To say I don't care about people's opinion of me would be false. I do care, but only to a certain degree. I now care more about how I feel about myself. If I'm judged harshly for being the absolute best person I can be, I can accept the criticism as people being "haters". But if I am in the wrong or I know that their opinions have truth to it. I'll make the necessary changes.

I can credit my little sister Krystle for showing me a real live example of the pure heart. If it wasn't for her I would forever think all humans are evil in some shape or form. Since I've known her (her whole life) I've never heard her speak ill of another person or treat anyone harshly. She has truly proved to me that there are such people in this world. My goal is to become one of them.

I want to attract those people in my life, motivate people to adopt that quality myself. It truly brings out the best in people when you can be righteous and display noble and morally sound qualities.

Brandon

The Reincarnation

People's beliefs on death differ drastically depending on what school of thought they study at or what their personal theories may be. But it truly is all speculative, and we're not here to battle religious or debate philosophies so I'm going to tell you how high I "metaphorically" reincarnated myself.

Definition of reincarnation is the rebirth of the soul in a new body. Now let me break this down. During my life I have been greatly awed by the metaphysical, the spiritual and the occult. And though I've had my experiences with all the above I finally found myself back at the physical, still searching for the keys of life. It was here that I needed to correct myself. Like I stated previously I was nonchalant about life because I felt like none of it mattered. Life was just a huge mystery that I didn't want to solve. I just thought I would leave all that to Scooby Doo and the gang. Not really, but I wasn't concerned with earthly matters, I was too busy searching for the keys to the universe when I was yet to find the simple keys to life. So, I continued to crash into walls. And that eventually led myself to prison to pull myself out of the stars and learn the lessons I needed to before moving on. The lesson I was to learn was righteousness and how to conduct myself accordingly.

I was busy searching for God and he revealed him/herself in a simple form. I eventually looked in the mirror and seen God looking back at me.

At this stage in my life I believe I was in purgatory. Somewhere along the line I died physically ended up in this temporary place of punishment to reflect on all my wrongdoings. I was forced to examine every little thing I did and had to figure out what was the right way before I can move to a better place.

I said this was a metaphoric analogy but when I recite it, it truly feels like a literal reincarnation.

For a while I was really all the way out of it. On the infamous acid trip that changed my life I feel like I really died. At some point I even believe myself to be a ghost. It was a terrible time in my life. I was distraught, disorganized, and confused. I didn't understand what I had done to inherit this miserable outcome.

For years I felt like I was in hell. These were the worst times I can remember it seemed nobody loved or cared for me. I felt completely alone. Trapped in an eternity of misery and enigma; puzzles I would never find answers to.

But I didn't give up. Though I was in this hell I wasn't going to let it destroy me. I would fight my way out of this place if it was the last thing I did and that's exactly what I proceeded to do. It was a terrible journey, filled with sticky situations and formidable adversaries but I had it set in my mind that I would be triumphant.

So, I fought. I fought until I won. I fell down but got up. I wouldn't take no for an answer and eventually I arrived. I had to recreate myself in order to proceed down the road to the blissful heavens that I have fought so dearly for.

My life was like a fantasy book, I had to conquer hideous demons who try to trick and deceive me at every turn. I had to push my feelings aside in order to complete the task at hand. I even had to discern reality from the phantasmal illusions to try to confuse and conformed to be. But I finally made it. My spirit was finally reformed in a new body and renowned mind. I've become invincible. I became a God.

What does it mean to become a God? The answer is controversial, but I'll elaborate from my perspective. Becoming a God is simple. It just means living life to your fullest potential, embracing yourself and others and seeing the universe as it truly is. Understanding the nature of things, adapting, and adjusting when necessary. Becoming a God means living in truth, displaying an unshakable fortress of morals and virtues, and remaining steadfast and vigilant. Gods aren't whimsical or fickle; they are sure and saved. Once a God, you will be worthy of admiration and you will become venerated. People will flock to your presence and seek your wisdom seeing the light that shines from within. In short, becoming a God is just alleging yourself with a higher power. In the Bible passage John 10:33–36 Jesus was escorted by the Pharisees. They claimed Jesus blasphemed by making himself a God. Jesus retorted "Is it not written in your law I said: you are gods." Then he went on to ask him something along the lines of "do you say I'm blaspheming for saying I'm the son of God when your scripture tells us we are all gods to?" This made their attack invalid because they clearly didn't understand the law and Jesus proved this to them with a few simple words. They wanted to persecute him for his righteous deeds and because he shed his light on their incompetence.

In all of us lives a hidden potential and once found and embraced we unlock our divinity and take what's rightfully ours. A throne in the Halls of Peace. Some may have different names or titles for this process, but I like to refer to it as the Becoming. Now my personal experience consisted of a deep yearning for the truth. I dedicate my life to vigorously searching for the thing that would end all suffering and provide me with the luxuries of wisdom and discernment. These gifts may not seem like much to one who views things only on the surface. They may appear as versus only for the old, gray-haired man, that can't be attained until you reach the "Golden Years" of your life. Contrarily, this is far from the truth. The wisdom is gained through experience we happen to experience reality every second of every day of our life. The application of the lessons learned is where wisdom and discernment come into play. This is where I found enlightenment. "A man may possess all the knowledge in the universe, but he will remain a fool if he doesn't play it."

With that being said I consider myself pretty knowledgeable, but my use of this knowledge was poor. And the things I concerned myself with weren't of relevance to the world I found myself in. So, while others were focused and leaving, I was too busy focused on what happens after life. I was busy trying to figure out something that wasn't relevant at the time and this is what led to my demise.

Though I believe I was righteous, I remained selfish trapped in a delusion to self-fulfillment. This is the reason I started experimenting with drugs. I believe an altered consciousness would allow me to receive the inside that I sought for so earnestly. Though it did alter my thought pattern and gave me what I believed to be a heightened awareness, it pulled me away from the truth. I was trapped in a self-induced coma, meta-phonetically speaking of course, that kept me stagnant.

Now did I learn anything from this experience? Of course, I learned to refocus my life on the here and now. Life after death "if it truly exists" wouldn't be too bad if I was doing the right thing. And though I believed I was doing the right thing my actions didn't show it.

I was scared of doing but I knew I needed to be doing. I was self-destructive, destroying every good opportunity that presented itself. I lacked the courage to make a true stand for what I believed was right. I feel like Jonah, and this prison is my modern-day whale. But unlike Jonah I was thankful for any revelation when it came. I embraced the change knowing I was a God Send. I began discarding all the bad traits I found myself possessing and proceeded to straighten the ones that I valued.

I grew strong. Less combative and more subtle I quit arguing and just listened. In my heart of hearts gathered a piece that would stand the test of time. It was exactly what I was looking for.

Remember the dream I related about running through hell and finally reaching heaven? Well, it played out in real life. Now I am untouchable, I am not rattled by the wicked thoughts and ramblings of the wrongdoer. I am comfortable and secure in my own kingdom. I see the beauty in all creation and admire the divine design. I want to be an example to the people that are like me. Together we will drive! We must all strive to attain this piece that so easily loses us. It starts first with self. Look at your life through a magnifying glass, so to say, and correct every little thing that you dislike about yourself. Search inwardly for your truth and take back your respect. Life is to live! We weren't here to be mediocre, and this I had to learn for myself. Now that I've recreated myself, my outward appearance and my inward thought pattern, I no longer believe in impossibilities.

I was to have a mental blockage that wouldn't allow me to push my limits. All the things I believe I was capable of doing were just dreams that I entertained. I feel like if I tried these things, I would fail completely so I unconsciously sabotage myself. I destroyed every opportunity to excel and continued to live my life in a constant revolving circle that was conducive to an unwanted emotional state.

Now that I've taken my life back, I have a mentality that nothings too far out of reach. I can literally do anything I put my mind to, or at least give it a good shot. With this sound mind I become fearless. There is no obstacle enough to thwart my plans. If I see it and want it, I will have it. Nothing can keep me away from my goal. Therefore, I must focus my purpose on attaining everything I desire. If not achieved I will feel like my task is incomplete, so I resolve to push myself to the limit. Give each and everything I set my mind on the utmost respect it deserves and see it through to the end.

All the things that I wish for is feasible. I realize now that I hold myself to a higher standard. At the recreating myself I noticed I was just working at the bottom of the food chain, desperate and lonely, satisfied with nothing. I was pitiful and didn't see a way out of my agony.

But now that all that is out of the window, success is mandatory. Now that the barriers have been broken there's no looking back. The best is all I think of all I talk about, all I know.

Looking at TV I see all the possibilities. There are so many men and women who are employed through this medium alone. From actors, editors, screen writers, and costume designers.

Hundreds of thousands of jobs and opportunities. That's just talking about the movies, commercials, and TV shows. What about the models, fashion designers, and photographers? Or the book editors, promoters, and distributors? There is truly unlimited potential out there to be exactly what you want to be. All it takes is your drive and motivation.

Are you going to make excuses why you didn't go to practice or skip school? Or are you going to suck it up and push through to the finish line? It's all up to you! You have the ability to live your best life no matter what your circumstances may be. Just look at me. I chose to change my whole lifestyle around and live like a God on Earth. And this book is a product of my efforts and my struggles. Everyday Chris and I help strengthen each other. Steel sharpens steel and birds of a feather, flock together. I reincarnated myself for the better, now it's your turn!

Chapter 13

Christopher

Critical Analysis

Selling drugs is what brought me into the penal system. I can even say that Deidre is the cause of my incarceration because she sent the police my way. Which is how I got caught with the weed. That will not only be a lie, but it will also be a disservice to myself for wasting time, energy and thought in the wrong direction. The true cause for every single thing I've been through is myself. That is the only way to truly analyze the situation.

Everything that happens can be traced back to yourself. The way people treat you, the things you go through, all of it comes back to you. Even the things you cannot control, you can always control your mind and how you process the situation.

Perfect peace or total distraught is a condition of your own mind. Some will spend their whole incarceration blaming others for the reason they are in prison. They sound like the villains from Scooby Doo "I would have gotten away with it, if it weren't for you meddling kids!" And just how the villains from Scooby Doo sound foolish, so do you. If you were never doing anything illegal from the start, no one will have anything to tell on.

Even though I'm in prison for weed charges and weed is now legal. I cannot fool myself into thinking that is my only problem or area I have to focus on. The charge itself means nothing. It's the thought pattern of the man who got caught that needs to be analyzed. Because if I didn't go down for this, it would have easily been for something else.

I have an unwanted gigantic hundred-year-old oak tree planted firmly in my yard that I desperately want removed. I cannot waste time picking leaves off the tree or breaking off little miscellaneous branches. I would be wasting precious energy and time on doing trivial insignificant cosmetics on the tree, but it will still be strongly planted. I must dig beneath the surface and remove the tree from the roots. Any other methods will not suffice, and the tree will grow back. I want it totally dislodged forever.

The analytical process is very crucial and conducive to the enrichment of my life. There is not one successful entity that I know of that does not have people assigned to the analyzing process. Sports, weather, businesses, churches, schools, military services, nature, industries, and politics. Everything requires an analysis. When you closely examine and figure how the elements work and function you then gain insight and enlightenment. Enabling you to make improvements.

I've come to realize that our lives are functioning bodies that require due diligence, maintenance, and repairs on a constant basis.

I cannot afford to "go with the flow" or just freestyle my way through life. That doesn't work well for me. When you go whichever way, the winds blow at you, you might end up getting blown into a prison or worse an early grave.

Through constant vigilance I can ensure a life of freedom, liberty, and prosperity. Some people are different, they can live through their lives with no real fear of legal issues because something in their mindset will never allow them to act upon certain thoughts. While analyzing myself, I realized I am not one of those people. I tend to act upon thoughts and impulses that I have, so I must constantly be aware of my thoughts.

The best athletes in the world are ranked as such because all they do is practice their craft, train, and analyze their performances so they can exploit their strength and improve on their weaknesses. Failure is a direct result of negligence. Learning this valuable lesson through experience, is why I now take time out of my day every day to meditate. It gives me an opportunity to examine, reflect, and ponder on my life. Within yourself you will find all the answers you seek. God has a way of speaking to you when you isolate yourself and seek truth and enlightenment.

Self-reliance is the key to analyzing yourself. When you seek the truth, you can and it is within yourself, if you are on the path of righteousness and strive for moral perfection. When you seek for others to analyze you, that leaves room for ill-intended criticism, skepticism, hypocrisy, and misguidance. I was once told by a wise man that, "He, who builds according to everyone else's advice, will have a crooked house". This statement could not have been any truer.

Everyone has the ability to formulate their own thoughts. We cannot force our beliefs and teachings upon others. With this in mind, the man who is not self-reliant and steadfast with his own thoughts and decisions can easily be swayed to each and every possible direction.

When you're on the path of nobility and you know you are doing the right thing, your own analysis is the only one that counts. It is you alone who has to live and account for every thought and action committed by you.

If you can analyze yourself successfully and keep yourself on the right path, it will eliminate the possibility of others having to judge you and do the analysis for you. Namely, the justice system. Me coming to prison, where I had to walk this journey alone. Showed me how to become self-reliant. The isolation gave me the much-needed space to gather my thoughts and awaken spiritually. The Zen I acquired was life changing and without God opening my eyes, I would have been forever lost.

With the advancement of technology and increasing use of social media, it has become exceedingly difficult for people to obtain absolute solitude and total isolation to spiritually awaken and create peace in their lives. It seems everyone is seeking "clout", approval, or direction from the next person.

I have worried about being released and getting caught in the whirlwind of the fast pace moving society. If I am not firm enough in my stance in life, I worry I will crumble and succumb to the worldly temptations that will surround me. The most clarity I've received in my life has been in the moments of solitary confinement. This fact at one time worried me because I don't want to have to be locked up in order to have Zen in my life!

The answer to this concern came to me through meditation. I can create a solitary environment for myself in the free world! You don't have to be removed from society forcibly by others, do it yourself. This revelation gave me great peace and joy because it gave me a definitive way to keep myself grounded and free.

I began spinning my wheels, coming up with endless scenarios where I can create a Zen like atmosphere. Going to church is a good option that I will explore, but the total solitude that I require will be activities such as: fishing, hiking, walking trails, going to the gym late at night, and camping. I've even thought of going to a hotel for a weekend every month or so, and just meditating. No phone, no tv, and no company. I've realized there are many possibilities and options that I can explore to keep up with the continual analysis of my life. In my case, living day by day in a rapid constant life without stopping to examine and check myself, leads to my life spiraling out of control. I also realized I was stubborn and didn't want to listen to my parents. I should have trusted their wisdom because their direction was in alignment with righteousness, whereas mine was not, at the time. Now that I am morally sound and on the continual path of righteousness, I can trust in myself to make the right decisions in life, that will lead me to peace, happiness, and prosperity.

Before I was awakened in phases I was a child. Even though one may be of the legal adult age, that doesn't constitute you being an adult. A child is dependent upon his/her parents for guidance, livelihood, and nurture. When you become a true adult, you can rely upon yourself. Peace and happiness cannot be given to you by no one other than yourself.

Some may argue that their kids are enough to make them happy, or money, or status in life. If that's the case why are there so many adults with kids, money or status in life still unhappy? True salvation, strength, peace, joy, and happiness must come first from within. After that, then the outer world will take shape to mirror the condition that lies within.

I've heard many times from various people that, "you cannot help anyone else, until you first take of yourself". How can you teach math, science, language art, sports, or anything if you, yourself don't know anything about it? Many people are in the pursuit of happiness. They search high and low and still cannot find it. I believe it is the wrong place. True happiness will come from within. That is what makes analysis so critical.

Brandon
Critical Analysis

If it wasn't for me being constructively self-criticizing, I wouldn't have made it this far. Every day I go hard on myself, harder than anyone else can go because I know what's going on in my head. I can judge my inner thoughts and be truly critical with my analysis. This provides a medium for the deepest retrospection but also requires a spirit of truth. With this spirit I judge myself honestly it can be content with the verdict because I know it's truly beneficial.

Just yesterday I woke up ready to make excuses for why I should lay back down and go back to sleep. I literally caught myself running through a bit of reasons to slack off. Immediately I eliminated that thought pattern and got up and put in work. Without the practice of critically analyzing I wouldn't have been able to notice where I was falling short at and would have continued in my folly. Thus, the subject matter of this chapter Critical Analysis.

Let's examine my life before the reincarnation from the perspective of no critical analysis. I've talked about my journey up until this point. Now I'm going to recount some events from an elevated viewpoint. I'll refer to two days as they shoulda, coulda, wouldas. Without this self-analysis I found myself in plenty of unfortunate situations.

For instance, if I never would have started experimenting with drugs, I probably wouldn't have found myself in prison. If I analyze my thought pattern and applied logic, I could have predicted the outcome. $1+1 = 2$. And drugs plus a lack of self-discipline equals a junkie underachiever, which I ended up becoming. If I simply would have used my mind, I would be in a much better position in life right now. But if I was a fifth, we would all be drunk. Right? Maybe, but obviously without using my mental facilities accordingly I found myself making ignorant decisions frequently. I didn't have a plan and the plans that I did have weren't well thought out. I was too busy searching for my next thrill instead of looking to the future.

When I did look to the future though it was vague. I tried not to focus on it because what I saw in the "Crystal ball" was ugly. I knew the choices and decisions I made were leading me down the path of self-destruction, so I did everything possible to avoid giving it any attention. Without correction, my future was looking rather bleak. And without the critical analysis, I had no way to correct it. So, I continued on in my ignorance and it eventually led me to a place where I had no choice but to self-correct. The Department of Corrections.

Now once again if I had applied this critical analysis concept to my relationships, I wouldn't have so many broken ones. When I sit here and think about why I have no friends "riding" with me, I have no choice but to blame myself. Why? Because if I was truly a friend,

I would have made sure that my friendships would last. The only way I could've done this was by being good to the people that cared for me but though I loved them, I was far from being good to them.

All I cared about was me, me, me! I was going to get my next meal, smoke my next blunt, or enjoy my next thrill. My life wasn't my life. I was too busy living in other people's shadows. I was a supporting role in a movie where I was supposed to be the lead actor. Everybody who I hung out with helped me, but they also handicapped me. Nobody ever told me to get up and make something out of my life. But they weren't supposed to. I should've done all of this myself. If I was as critical of myself about these matters as I am now, I will be in a way better place. But once again if it was a fight.

Critical analysis is imperative if you want to change your life around, but you will need to prepare for the ugly truth. When I look at my life, I see that I was truly a burden in society. I didn't have anything but a delusional positivity that I thought would save the world.

Now don't get me wrong, I wasn't just a complete bum, I definitely provided when possible and always did good deeds. I was just unaware of my shortcomings and unable to correct them. Year after year I entertained myself with this illusion and never once thought I would be able to share it. It's when I finally sit down and deeply analyze myself when the truth hit me. It hit me so hard that it knocked me out of the "mental coma" I found myself in. I was disgusted with the past and consequently started correcting it with vigor and enthusiasm.

I became nitpicky. Picking at every little detail including the most insignificant points in life. I became obsessed with change. It was definitely a work in progress. They require constant vigilance. I stayed on the watch and ready. Ready to take action at the quickest instant. I became a superhero, fighting off all the villains that thought it was a good idea to make my mind their evil lair. It is a strenuous process; constantly analyzing and reacting at the slightest sign of trouble. But it is also highly beneficial. Remaining alert, I am able to swiftly choose the correct course of action in any circumstance.

Let's think about a sports analyst. He breaks down every single detail in order to draw a conclusion. He then gives a summary on what he believes are the teams strengths and weaknesses. After critically analyzing the team, the coach can either choose to accept the analysis criticism or reject it. This is either to his rise or demise according to his decision to set on the analysis or ignore it.

I just imagine what it would be like to be constantly aware of your thoughts, good and bad. Would you continue to do what you knew was counterproductive or would you choose to change your thought patterns? Hopefully, you chose the latter. Some people may think doing this is an impossible task, but it just takes practice like everything else. If you can perceive it and you believe it, you can achieve it! Just like that! It really is simpler than it sounds. It only requires action. People talk about what is possible every day but with no action they make no progress. This I came to find through my own analysis of self. I can talk about a major game, but if I'm not making plays, I'm not getting paid.

My whole perspective on life has changed. Everything I do and stand for will be solid. My world will be final. If I say it, I mean it.

To continue in foolishness would make everything I said thus far invalid. I would be discarding one delusion for another. Who wants to live a lie? I certainly don't and this is the reason I chose to change. You know how the world thinks and judges. According to your actions, deeds, appearance, and other things. But it is in our own hands of what we give them to judge. If you're judging and criticizing yourself rigorously you leave little room for negative opinions to be formed. Granted, people remain people, and humans. So, there will always be someone with an ill formed opinion about you. But as long as you're hard on yourself, you know the truth and every day strive for perfection. Again, with this kind of mental attitude you've become an impenetrable force. You are not susceptible to other people's whims or fancies. You remain steadfast in your confidence, knowing that you are good to yourself and righteous in your walk. You build your house on a strong foundation while others build on sand.

Envision all the unnecessary danger you would avoid if conscious of your thoughts. You would no longer be controlled by your own environment, but you become the master of circumstance, controlling your surroundings. The people you attract will be a direct reflection of yourself. You will no longer find yourself burdened with a load too heavy to manage because it isn't in alignment with your being.

There is a universal law called the Law of Attraction. This law states that you will track whatever you focus your thoughts on whether positive or negative. I'm going to take the mysticism out of the equation and we're going to look at this from a logical standpoint.

If I continually thought and dwelled on a fancy sports car, how would I attract it? OK let's view this hypothesis from both the positive and negative perspectives. First, we have the positive scenario. Since I was young, I dreamed of owning a Lamborghini. My life wouldn't be complete if I never had the chance to personally possess this car. Knowing this and thinking about this car constantly, I would eventually align myself with whoever and whatever in order to reach this goal. Being a positive person and adhering to society's standards, I would get a job and work as hard as possible, constantly driven by my subconscious and the thing I want most in life. Working hard I would eventually get a promotion placing myself closer to my goal. This Lamborghini is constantly looming in the back of my mind though I'm not consciously focused on it. So, I continue to work. By the time I sit back and analyze where I'm at in life I noticed that I have accumulated enough money to make a down payment on a car of my dreams. Having a "will do" attitude and constantly taking time to analyze your life you will arrive at each and every goal you set.

Now we go to the opposite end of the spectrum. Let's say I had the same infatuation with this Lamborghini, but I was a pessimist and lazy. I have always thought about this Lamborghini, but I didn't put the proper work in to secure it by honest means. Though I loved this car and knew I had to have one, I sold drugs in order to arrive at my destination. The whole time I sold these drugs I had to worry about the police and going to jail, losing everything I work for. This for one is a detrimental mindset that will eventually cause me to topple. And now that I finally acquired this car the inevitable happens. Yes, I may have possessed the Lambo, but I wasn't able to enjoy it because while I had it I constantly worried about it being seized due to my illegitimate means of gaining the car. Now, if I wouldn't have taken time to analyze my life with the spirit of truth, I would have foreseen my downfall in adjusting my life accordingly.

These two examples show just how critical it is to self-analyze. It gives you an advantage over the people who continue to remain ignorant to the power of thought and correction. With this weapon harnessed you become a force to be reckoned with in the battlefield of life.

Chapter 14

Christopher

Freedom: The Mind State (Embracing Positivity)

Incarceration is defined as being confined, or a state of captivity. This is referring to a physical sense, meaning your spiritual or mental state was not included.

When I was sentenced to serve a few years of my life incarcerated, that did not include my happiness or my spiritual well-being. Those are things that cannot be touched by no other man or system. Sure, prison is not what one would typically call a happy place full of fun. But you've read my story and witnessed the great blessings I've received and trials I've overcome. From right where I sit, I was able to mend fracture relationships. (LaShonda, Elroy, Crockett, Tonya, Daysia, Adriane, Krystle, Timothy, Dewayne, and last but not least God!) I was also able to become a better man and gain enlightenment. These things brought a joy to me that I never even experienced in the free world. So, in retrospect, I can see where I've indeed received positive from a seemingly negative situation.

I was only sentenced to physically sit in a cell, nothing more. The hurt, pain, misery, violence, and distress were not a part of my

235

sentence. I don't recall hearing the judge say to me, "Mr. Oaks, I hereby sentence you to a life of misery!" Fortunately, he doesn't possess that power. Because if he did, I would be in a whole world of trouble!

Positivity alone is the main element that got me through the hell I was in. Positivity in my parents sending the book that helped save my life "Mind is the Master" Positive conversation on the vent put me in communication with Bad Wolf, which led to me reading "Millionaire Prisoner", which also gave me salvation and inspired me to write this book. The whole purpose of this book is to share my story, spread positivity, explore a legal avenue to make income, and do better for my kids. No matter the situation, a positive mindset can be achieved. If I can do it from a long-term isolation cell in prison, anyone can do it. For this, I am certain.

The wonderful thing about the mind is that no one can take it from you. It is the single thing in life in which you have total control over. Once you can take full ownership and responsibility for your mind, you cannot be stopped. Every situation can have either a positive or negative perspective. As the old cliché goes, "the glass is either half empty, or half full." However, you determine to evaluate it is up to you. It sounds easier said than done. I understand this however, when you continually look for the good in every situation you will receive extremely positive results! I strongly urge you to try it.

For example, my situation is that I am locked in the cell for 24 hours, 7 days a week in total isolation. I am not out there physically for my family, I have no "social" life, I get lonely, bored, and it would seem that I have nothing working in my favor. This is the obvious most basic way to look at this situation. Now let me paint the picture of positivity for you that I see. I am in an isolated space that allows me to meditate easily. Zen is an everyday occurrence. I have one thing that there is not enough of and can never be bought. The richest men on earth cannot buy what I have, that will be time! I can use this time to completely transform into a person who will succeed. I can use this time to be studious by reading, studying, and learning everything I can. I can use this time to write books and make money from my jail cell! I am not distracted by women, social media, TV daily tasks, or company. I am in a situation that if exploited properly, can elevate me to heights I've never been before. That opportunity was there the whole time, but with the wrong mindset and attitude, I would have never discovered it. All the precious opportunities and time that people waste just because of how a situation may appear is senseless. Remaining calm, positive, humble, patient, and creative will always put you in a winning situation. With a positive attitude and a solid hold over your mind, you gain freedom and inner peace. No one can subject you to being unhappy. Only you can determine how your attitudes, moods, and mental states are. Invite only positive into your life. Plant only seeds of sweet fruit, not sour. The result will be yielding the harvest you expected.

The strongest tool any man can possess is his brain. Under no circumstances can you let the next person control or manipulate your brain. That is the core of who you are. When you allow outer circumstances or other people to compromise your peace of mind, it renders you ineffective. A few tactics I use to help my mind stay positive and healthy is to alter my surroundings. The cell I am in once resembled a dungeon. It was dirty, uncomfortable to live in and uninviting to the eye. I at once had to change this by cleaning the cell from top to bottom. I use fruit scented shampoo to mop the floors and clean the walls, giving the cell a coconut-lime smell. I stack all of my books to give the cell character and I hang various pictures up to give me scenery. The pictures are everything from beach scenes to luxury cars and homes, beautiful women, flowers, animals, and pictures of my family. Keeping the cell and myself clean at all times is essential to my mind being relaxed and at ease. Using Muslim oils, I make "jail house" incents and I burn them in times of meditation and reading. All of those things enrich my atmosphere, allowing my mind to transcend prison. Although it may appear that I am in a prison cell, in thought, I am actually everywhere but, from a luxury New York office, to a penthouse suite in Miami Florida. With a little imagination it's amazing what the mind can do.

The technology we have today makes a lot of things possible that were not possible in the past. Business can be conducted online through emails. You can manage bank accounts online, you can promote, market, and sell products, all online. With the right support and people in your network, owning and operating legal businesses is possible to do from a prison cell. So, with this mindset every day I am in the office. Why not put in the work and become a workaholic? There is nothing but positive that can come from thinking this way.

I can give massive praise to Joshua Kruger, Mike Enemigo, and James Allen for opening my eyes and heart to the endless possibilities and opportunities that lie before me. The same is available to everyone. It all starts with yourself. You must embrace positivity, allowing it to flow through your bloodstream.

I was utterly lost at one point in my life. Lost to the point where I did not want to live anymore. I contemplated suicide numerous times. By the grace of God, I was saved. Love and positivity alone made everything possible. The unconditional love from my family kept me alive long enough to see the light! I witnessed firsthand how love and positivity saves lives. This is the driving force that made me want to share my story and put this book into production. If I can do for the next person what was done for me, then I can truly feel that I have indeed paid my debt to society.

Brandon

Freedom the Mind State

(Embracing Positivity)

What does it mean to be free? This is all based on one's opinion. There are many definitions of freedom but the one that stood out to me reads as follows: freedom- the ability to act without undue hindrance or restraint. To me this is the best definition. Yeah, I may be incarcerated and some of my rights may be temporarily suspended but that does not deprive me of my spirit. My spirit remains free and I am able to thrive in my environment and know that no one can truly take my freedom away. I still possess the freedom to act without undue hindrance knowing that I am acting in accordance with justice and choose to do what's right. This is the only thing that holds any relevance in these would be times of distress.

Do I miss women, eating good food and playing video games? Of course! But what good American man wouldn't? Do I live in a facility with controlled movements? My captors weren't able to strip me of my imagination. I live in paradise though the people around me are miserable. I'm at the beach because other people are in gladiator school. I eat luxuriously while my peers complain about the kitchen food. Why is this? Because freedom is a mind state not something one can give and take away at will. No! Freedom is universal! If you have the power to control your mind, then you have the power to be free in whatever ordeal or dilemma you find yourself in.

This book is written in real time so as I continue to grow you are along on my journey with me. With that in mind, check this out. Just about five days ago I ate a couple of fire balls, a prison staple, I enjoyed them though they were extra hot. Little to my knowledge they were a little too hot. I woke up the next morning and my tongue was raw. It was extremely painful to eat and would have ruined my week if I allowed it to. But do you know what I did? I refuse to let my sore tongue damper my mood. No, when I find myself trying to complain I merely replaced it with the mantra of a faithful Christian, "This too, shall pass! And to pass it did, I had to make adjustments to my thoughts. Instead of falling victim to my circumstance, I controlled it with the power of free thought. Actually, when I spoke about making excuses not to get up in the morning and work a sore tongue was among the horde.

According to Albert Einstein "imagination is more important than knowledge. Knowledge of limited imagination encircles the world" This quote holds major weight with me, because without imagination the world would never evolve. What if no one ever imagined harnessing electricity? Where would we be? Somewhere still lighting candles. Worrying about burning down the village because of a stray ember? Exactly! We wouldn't be men and women, boys and girls without the beautiful power of imagination.

We possess this beautiful gift, so we must use it accordingly. Let's not waste this freedom imagining things that are detrimental. Let's use it in a way that is constructive. Let's imagine the world as a better place and take the steps to transmute this from our minds into our reality.

Nobody is ever free from restrictions. People are always held to a certain code of conduct determined by society. If these rules are broken and they will find themselves in my current position. Confined. A lot of people attend this outcome and come under the pressure. I was almost one of them. When I first came to prison, I held a rebellious stance. I wouldn't allow the system to tame me, not seeing the benefits of being evil. I was like a wild animal running around fighting and lashing out at my captors. I thought they were trying to deprive me of my manhood, but I was just yet to find it. But after continuous revolutions down an evil spiral I had to break the pattern which led me here to this point. True freedom.

I know that I can't just hop in a car and drive across the country, but I can imagine it. And with my imagination and my action I can bring this dream to life by aligning myself with the things I know I need in order to make the journey, money, car, maps, planning. It is all feasible. But doing the things I know I need to be doing is what makes it factual. So why live your life in a negative manner? We've discussed the law of attraction. Are you happy with attracting negativity or do you want the best outcome possible? Of course, you want the best, so let's switch it up!

Now let's compare and contrast a "can-do" attitude with a "will do" attitude.

The difference between "can do" and "will do" are like black and white, hot, and cold and day and night. "Can do" means just that "can-do". It's possible to do anything you put your mind to. I can be the Emperor of the World, but will I be is the question. Can implicates a possibility. But it indicates I will get up today and work hard beats every time. "Can do" is the first step though. If you know you can do anything, you are a step ahead of those who don't know. The more you realize you're able to attain the more knowledge you possess. But here's where the wisdom comes in. You know the right thing you should be doing but will you do it or remain in the wide spectrum of possibilities. Choose wisely.

Negativity. It just sounds nasty. When I first came in contact with this word, I was young and in school. I was in my pre-algebra class and was learning about integers namely negative numbers. If you look at a number line zero being in the middle, you will find the negative numbers on the left and the positive on the right of zero. Knowing how my mind works I immediately associated these negative numbers with loss. And it makes perfect sense to me. If the surface of the water is zero would you rather be at one or -1

243

considering there was a bunch of hungry sharks in the vicinity. Being at -1 in this situation is sure to lead to a negative situation; one you don't want to be in. When my bank account is in the negative, I'm in debt. When I have a negative attitude, I am subtracting from the positive experience I would be enjoying. From these examples I draw my conclusion. Negativity sucks the life out of everything. Do you like being around people who are constantly complaining? Or those that don't have anything good to say? I surely don't. Why? Because they kill the mood and make every situation uncomfortable. With the mental freedom that I possess I choose to remain in high spirits in every situation I experience, enjoying the height of ecstasy and remaining blissful.

Negativity is not conducive to the environment I am pursuing. If I want a good life, where does negativity fit in? Hmm... Good question! In order to live an exceptional life, one must have balance. Being an optimist, I tend to see everything with a positive eye.

Another valuable lesson I've learned in algebra class is this, if you subtract a negative number from a positive number you end up turning that negative into a positive and the problem turns into an additionthink problem. For example, 5-(-5) = 10. Understanding this mathematical expression and applying it to life, I go from having a negative thought to subtracting it, which just adds positive thoughts. With this practice I can't lose, this is nothing but room for growth. Negativity is just unnecessary! It's not needed in life and for those who find themselves in negative environments just start adding happy thoughts and actions and eventually you will climb yourself out of that bad place.

Once you fully embrace your positivity your life will change drastically. Just look at my example. I went from chump to champ. After all the losses I've taken I finally began winning in life. I won my self-respect back. I won my willpower. I want my peace of mind. I fought hard enough so I deserve it. At least in my own opinion. But I wouldn't have been able to do it if it wasn't for positivity. If I was never speaking about positivity on the vent, I never would have met Christopher. Reading his section, we already know what his first opinion of me was. But you never know something until you truly know it. And what I truly know is positivity saves lives, because it saved me and allows me to gain my freedom back. My true freedom! The freedom to be. Thank you, God and universe, master, and slave, for you truly revealed the way of righteousness to me and allow me to embrace positivity! Free at last!

Chapter 15

Christopher

Using your Mind, the Time is Now!

Freedom of thought and freedom of expression can lead to much confusion and controversy. This can make it difficult for even the most earnest seeker of truth to find a solid rock of refuge. This is because the world we live in is filled with controversial notions, causing many to be lost, not knowing which way to go.

In the midst of all the confusion, the beautiful simplicity of the answers lies upon the truth. Truth is based on and surrounded by facts. Controversy is based and surrounded by hypotheses. A fact is fixed and final. A hypothesis is a variable with vanishing suppositions. When seeking for the truth, in any capacity, whether it be the court system, relationships, parents, schools, businesses or spirituality, the only element that needs to be sought out are the facts. Identifying the facts and making decisions based upon those facts will give you the truth in which you were seeking.

There are two facts that I want to identify. Man is and as he thinks, so he is. Those two facts alone prove that your mind is the center of who you are and being that no one can think for you unless you allow them to have the power to change yourself and your circumstances at will. There is no set time to take full ownership of your mind. The perfect time is now! The only time that truly exists and is tangible is the present. The past is history, and the future is a later fantasy that doesn't exist in the now. When you make plans for the future, you only hope things go according to your plan. Who would have planned or foreseen the Covid-19 to interfere with the lives of everyone in the world? Tomorrow is not promised; therefore, you must live for the now. Yes, plan and set goals for the future, for Rome wasn't built overnight. I am referring to the condition of your mind, your happiness, joy, peace, imagination, creativity, and your spiritual growth. That all starts now. When you can do this successfully you are truly living.

What good is life itself if you cannot take joy, be happy, spread love, experience beauty, and evolve? When I lacked all of those traits, I had no desire to live. It is especially important to understand that all of those conditions are in your immediate reach and sphere. Happiness is not some external thing that needs to be sought out. It is the internal awakening of your heart and spirit. That is a fact! External and material things bring momentary pleasure and gratification. Those feelings are nice and enjoyable however, if you seek that constant joy, peace, harmony, and growth you must take a look from within and focus all of your energies in that direction.

Once your mind is in a healthy state you can then use it to unlock an unlimited number of doors. Opportunity is only limited to your imagination. Having a positive open mind allowed me to discover opportunities where I previously thought never existed. Knowledge, love, support, humanity, peace, joy, selflessness, patience, hard work, determination, dedication, and spiritual growth are all major keys to success that unlocks doors, and everyone has access to those very keys. Start with yourself. Eat, breathe, and sleep positivity and the universe will reciprocate this unto you.

Man cannot be separated from his mind; his life cannot be separated from his mind; his life cannot be separated from his thoughts. Mind, thought, and life are inseparable as fish gills, and water. Man, as mind is subject to change. He is not something "made" and finally complete but has inside him the potential for progress. By the universal law of evolution, he has become what he is, and is becoming that which he will be. His existence is altered by every thought he thinks. Every experience affects his character. Every effort made sways his mentality. These are facts of life that are fixed and final. Self-destruction or salvation are results caused by your own actions. This understanding should bring you peace. No longer must you blame or worry about your circumstances being the results of an unknown force that is beyond your control.

To live in a world full of excuses, blame, procrastination, and unaccountability, is to live in a world of folly. No true happiness is to be gained by living in folly. Reflecting on my life and seeing how far I have come, has convinced me of one thing I never thought was true before-redemption. I never thought I had a caring, understanding, or a forgiving heart because I didn't believe people could change. My view was that there were just certain kinds of people in the world and that's just the way it was. I limited myself as being one of those people who was just prone to being a "street hustler" and a "trapper", doomed for a life behind bars and a world full of constant lows and momentary highs.

Long before I ever came to prison, my mind was chained and confined, and long before my release date, I gained my freedom. There are many individuals in the world who are physically free, but mentally are held in captivity- a mental prison. My desire and goal are to help you locate that inner key and free yourself! No one has the authority to rule your mind or sentence you to any amount of unhappiness. You're the only one truly responsible for your actions. Take ownership now!

Brandon

Using Your Mind, the Time Is Now!

The ultimate powers we have at our disposal are the powers of our mind and the powers of now. With these two facilities harnessed there remains nothing that can stand in our path and hinder us from our success. You have been in the passenger seat as I embarked on the journey to self-transformation. It's been a crazy, emotional and healing experience. As I write this right now, I can tell you I reached my destination. I am the man that I've wanted to be my whole life. In this aspect I am hugely successful. Now comes the finances. But with the spirit in accordance everything else will topple at my feet like dominoes.

The only reason I was able to be successful in finding myself is because I used the two ultimate powers to my benefit. I truly evaluated life and singled out the areas I fell short in. With the power of mind, the finest weapon a man can possess if well-tuned. I used logic to correct my thought pattern. And no, I didn't procrastinate I took advantage of the now. Doing this allowed me to evolve rapidly. It was all a matter of devotion. Do I want this or not? The answer was yes! I wanted the change, so I sought it energetically. At every single turn in life I was searching, I knew there had to be a better way and finally I acquired the thing I desire mostly. Myself!

The powers of the mind are invaluable, you can't put a price on them. There is no force on earth that compares to it. With the power of mind, a nation can rise. With this same power a nation can, be destroyed. So, what are we to do with this great force? Use it. Use it to the best of our abilities. Experiment with it, play with it, and come to know it. It is the best thing you can ever do for yourself.

Imagine going from lazy to productive; unorganized to highly efficient; from depressed to ecstatic. These are all within your reach. With the power of the mind you have the ability of choice. You make the decisions about what you think, believe, and know. You have the power to get up and go to work or call in. You have the power to exercise or eat potato chips and drink pop all day. The decision is ultimately up to you.

Yesterday I made myself get up out of bed and stay up because I know changing my schedule would be more productive. They say the early bird gets the worm and if the worm is then dollars then I'm going to make myself that early bird. Why? Because I have the power to make myself do anything, I need to do it doesn't matter if I have to stand up all day. If I want to achieve my goal, I will do whatever it takes. It all starts with the decision. Allow your decision to be final immediately by any means.

Another power of the mind is the thoughts we think. It may not seem like it, but we are in control of everything we think, say, and do. There is no one to blame for the moods we find ourselves in or the situations. We can easily change the things we think of. It all starts with becoming conscious of our thoughts.

At every second of the day we are thinking of something whether we are aware of it or not. Once you understand this fact and begin examining your thoughts then you become capable of changing them. You can dwell on bad things and what could have been all day but that's exactly what you will get bad things and nothing. Or you can dwell on good things and what will be. And you can expect them to manifest. Good things are to be enjoyed and bad things are to be avoided. So, you must make the conscious effort to focus on all the good things in life.

Count your blessings. There are more things to rejoice about and few things to mourn over. Being positive you will attract positive things in your life. Likewise, with negativity. So, smile, enjoy life and Marvel at the wonders. Just be happy!

Now, with every little thought we are emitting a slight vibration. When our brain is functioning, it is firing messages back and forth like a text message and these are picked up by our synopsis. Just as your voice radiates a strong vibration, your thoughts emit a more subtle form of the same vibration. If you call someone's name, they are unconsciously altered to this sound. Well this same principle applies to the vibrations of thought. With every little thought we have we are attracting an outcome into our life with those tiny vibrations until it finally manifests in our reality. With that being said, we want to eat, sleep, and breathe positivity. Because we want the good things in life.

Now the energy we use thinking can be used to our advantage or our downfall. Every day we have energy to expand. Are you going to use it recklessly allowing your subconscious to lead your thoughts here and there, or are you going to take control and be productive? It's your prerogative. I know when I look back at my past, I see a lot of energy that I wasted on trivial things that weren't relevant to my growth. Every day I was thinking about my next high or something else that was going to aid me in remaining stagnant. But every once in a while, the thought of change wandered through my mind. I eventually began dwelling on it until it consumed my world. After all the energy I wasted, I finally made a conscious effort to put my energy to use and build a comfortable future. I was so tired of living like a stray dog. This is why I embraced the name "Bad Wolf." Though I remain wild, I am regal. You can put me in a cage, but you can't take my spirit away. Some may say Bad Wolf is a contradiction to everything I've spoken about, but it is actually an acronym for beautiful, artistic, dedicated, and devoted. My energy is constantly focused on positivity. I believe in truth, love, and justice and this is what I believe should saturate my life. I'm always conscious of the good in life in my subconscious program to it as well.

Programming your subconsciousness is a great way to help influence your conscious thoughts. I do this by placing pictures of things that I want to accumulate in my life. I also placed power words on the walls around me that are always visible. Words like win, succeed and thrive have all been on my cell walls at various times. Being ever present these words help program my subconscious thoughts to positivity. I find myself reading them randomly throughout the day. Reading them leads to thinking about them. Thinking about these words leads to acting upon them, which eventually leads to acquiring the fruits of my labors.

So, programming your subconscious is just another tool to help sharpen your mind, the ultimate weapon. Doing this will ensure that life's difficulties are conquered time and time again. Let's turn our focus on the power of now. Now is the present moment we find ourselves in. We should treat the now like a present, a gift from the creator to work toward our ultimate goal. Would you squander a precious gift from God? Hopefully not. I know I have squandered my fair share of gifts from God. I feel like this was complete disrespect towards the master of the universe. But being aware of this negligence, I diligently strive to never waste another moment of precious time.

The time is now! What am I doing now to create the best possible outcome for the future? I am currently working the hardest I've ever worked in order to secure my blessings. I meditate deeply, and search for anything I can accomplish at the present moment that will get me closer to my goal. Every second is opportunity and I plan on using every working minute to my benefit.

Yeah, every day is a struggle, we won but we aren't on the path of righteousness with you in your will and you will encounter people who will choose to press your buttons intentionally. But using the power of your mind and the power of now, you can always react with wisdom and thwart the plans of your enemy. In the Bible there's a scripture that goes along the lines of the devil walks about like a roaring lion seeking to devour you. I don't know how accurate that is, but you get the gist. There are many negative people walking around seeking to take away your peace because they are yet to attain theirs. But if you live in the now and count your blessings there is nothing the devil can do because you know you are truly safe in the calm controlled confines of your mind. You can choose to either allow someone else to control your mood or you can be your own master.

Life is psychological. If you understand the mind, then you understand people. If you understand the mind consequently you will understand yourself. Don't wait for next week to ask the girl of your dreams out. If you're ready, do it now. Christopher told me one thing that will stick with me for the rest of my life and that's "excuses are useless." I could make excuses for everything but where would they get me. If it's possible to do at that moment, do it.

Prioritize. Wield the unstoppable force of mind. Harness the quickly fleeting power of now and win in life. If I didn't practice what I preached I wouldn't be here talking to you. And just think.... it all started with Conversations Through The Vent.